REMARKS ON THE SONNETS OF SHAKESPEARE; WITH THE SONNETS. SHOWING THAT THEY BELONG TO THE HERMETIC CLASS OF WRITINGS, AND EXPLAINING THEIR GENERAL MEANING AND PURPOSE

Published @ 2017 Trieste Publishing Pty Ltd

ISBN 9780649690008

Remarks on the Sonnets of Shakespeare; With the Sonnets. Showing That They Belong to the Hermetic Class of Writings, and Explaining Their General Meaning and Purpose by William Shakespeare

Edited by Trieste Publishing Pty Ltd.
 Cover @ 2017

www.triestepublishing.com

WILLIAM SHAKESPEARE

REMARKS ON THE SONNETS OF SHAKESPEARE; WITH THE SONNETS. SHOWING THAT THEY BELONG TO THE HERMETIC CLASS OF WRITINGS, AND EXPLAINING THEIR GENERAL MEANING AND PURPOSE

ADVERTISEMENT.

For the convenience of those who may be drawn to
the study of the Sonnets of Shakespeare by these Remarks, the Author has given directions to print the
Sonnets with them.

E. A. H.

WASHINGTON CITY, D. C., Nov. 1864.

REMARKS

ON THE

SONNETS OF SHAKESPEARE.

———•••———

CHAPTER I.

HERMETIC writing is a species of painting; and as no artist upon canvas can be permitted to interpret his own picture, so no artistic hermetic writer can be allowed to translate into didactic statements the meaning of his own scripture or writing. It would be disgraceful for a painter to label a picture "this is a horse," to guard against its being mistaken for some other animal; and so, in like manner, if an art-writer, like Dante or Goethe, were to set about interpreting his own writings, it would be proof that his labors had fallen short of their object.

But while this is true with respect to the artist himself, it is entirely proper for a critic to discuss

and explain or exhibit, the meaning of artistic labors
in any of the fields of art, painting, music, sculpture,
architecture, or literature.

The highest performances of art reach far beyond
the ordinary judgments of man, and remain, for
most people, like mountain-tops, to which they are
often compared (as Mounts Sinai, Horeb, and Cal-
vary), almost inaccessible, where, nevertheless, the
atmosphere is always serene, like a beatified soul in
the presence of God.

Such performances of art seem to call for the
labors of a subordinate class of persons, who are not
artists themselves, but who have attained to such
discernment in art as to enable them, as it were, to
stand between the every-day life of the general current of men, and the higher expressed develop-
ments of genius, and by pointing out the scope or
inner meaning of great works of art, make them
appreciable to those who have not had their attention turned to them.

Such appreciation, however, would be impossible
if there were not something in common between the
highest order of genius, and the subtle pervadings
which bind all mankind in a brotherhood as fixed as
the everlasting principles of truth.

There are so many forms of hermetic writing in the world, that it is next to impossible to give any definition by which they may be distinguished. It may indeed be asserted that they all aim to illustrate life; and life may therefore be said to be the secret of all that class of writings; but no one, by this sort of statement, can be at once placed in a condition to enter into the true sense of the writings themselves, since to do this a knowledge of the secret is necessary; and who can lay claim to that knowledge without subjecting himself to the charge of arrogance and presumption?

Here the story of the philosopher occurs to us, who, being asked what God is, requested a day to think before answering, and then another, and another day, finally acknowledging that the more he thought of the question, the more difficult he found it to answer.

So is it with life. It is in us and around us, visible in myriad forms, but in itself invisible; and who can say he knows what life is? It is presupposed in both the question and the answer any one may give, and this, too, whether the answer be affirmative or negative—whether we assume to define it, or, confounded with a sense

of the mystery, we deny all knowledge of it.
We cannot hide ourselves from it; it is with us
in our hopes and our fears, in our joys and our
sorrows.

When we fully appreciate the difficulties of the
problem, the question may insinuate itself into
the mind, that is, into our sense of life, May not
one answer serve for both questions,—what is God,
and what is Life ?

And just here a student of this subject may be
in a fair position for inquiring into some of the
forms in which hermetic writers have treated
their subject, and especially the Sonnets attributed
to Shakespeare; and now we declare it to be our
purpose to show something of the meaning of those
exquisitely beautiful, but still more wonderful
Sonnets.

The question has long been agitated, as to whom
those Sonnets were addressed ; but no modern editor,
with whose labors we are acquainted, appears to
have considered for a moment that they belong to
the class of hermetic writings having a profoundly
mysterious sense, and no one seems to reflect that
perhaps they cannot be explained or understood
from any merely literal point of view. The efforts

of all of the critics appear to have been to discover to whom, as a person, the Sonnets were addressed; and the general opinion has been, that it was a young Earl,' the Earl of Southampton. This opinion was recently strongly urged in the April number of the London Quarterly Review for this year (1864). We think we can show, beyond the possibility of a doubt, that this solution of the problem presented in the Sonnets is entirely untenable; and this shall follow as a necessary inference from the exhibition we propose to make of the real object addressed, and we will show this from the Sonnets themselves.

That the Sonnets present a problem, as yet unsolved, not only appears from the article on Shakespeare and his Sonnets in the Review just named, but from the many discussions to be found in the various editions of the poet's works whenever the editors have anything at all to say on the subject. Thus, in a recent edition, the editor remarks, " If we could once discover the true solution of that *enigma* which lies hidden in the Sonnets attributed to Shakespeare, we might perhaps learn much that is now mysterious in the history of his life." *   In

* Hazlitt's edition.

1*

another place the same editor gives the opinion, that "his (Shakespeare's) Sonnets were probably among his earliest productions; but when they were written, where, and to whom they were addressed, and of whom they discourse, are all matters of mystery."

In the explanation we propose to make of the mystery, it is not denied but that many of the Sonnets have all the appearance of having been addressed to persons, sometimes to a man, and then again to a woman; and if this class of Sonnets stood alone they would not invite a mystical interpretation; but as they are found in a collection embracing a considerable number which cannot be understood as addressed to persons, while, at the same time, they admit of a decisive interpretation from what may be called the mystical theory, which may also without violence be applied to those apparently addressed to persons, it may properly be contended that the latter class are mystical also.

Love is a generic word, and we understand very well that the love of God is not only consistent with the love of man, but always includes and presupposes it; for which reason it is best figured under some special form of the love of man or woman.

This must explain why so many truly religious
works appear to the eye as mere love-stories, which
were intended to express the divine affection itself.
The love of art also participates in the highest form
of the affection, when its action is not corrupted by
the mere love of the reputation of an artist, just as
the love of knowledge tends to wisdom when it is
loved for itself and not merely for its temporal ad-
vantages.

We expect to show that love, as used in the
Shakespeare Sonnets, had not a mortal being for its
object, but an irrepresentable spirit of beauty, the
true source of artistic *births*.

Before proceeding to the point we aim at, let us
remark that, about the age of Queen Elizabeth, it
was quite common for poets to write series of sonnets, generally love-sonnets, apparently addressed to
some lady, in the fashion of Petrarch in an earlier
age, whose sonnets were addressed to Laura—said
to have been the wife of a dear friend of the poet!
Spenser wrote love-sonnets entitled, significantly
enough, Amoretti; and among the poets of that
age we find that Drayton published a series of sonnets dedicated to *Lilia*, in the preface to which he

holds this language,—" If thou muse what my Lilia is, take her to be some Diana, at the least chaste, or some Minerva; no Venus, fairer far. It may be she is Learning's Image, or some heavenly wonder which the precisest may not mislike : perhaps under that name I have shadowed Discipline."

Drayton published another series of sonnets besides those addressed to Lilia, which he expressly called " Ideas."

The first remark to be made upon Drayton's intimation in his preface to Lilia, and upon the fact that he entitled a series of sonnets *Ideas*, is, that we may take leave to suppose he was not alone, in the fact that he wrote sonnets, apparently addressed to a lady, which were, in truth, a series of idealistic contemplations upon various subjects of life; and we may use this preface of Drayton's in explanation of the sonnets of other poets of the age in which they were written; for we all know that literature has its fashions like everything else.

Among the poets of that age, or about it, Sir Philip Sidney is to be numbered. He published a series of sonnets entitled Astrophel and Stella; and no one can read them carefully without perceiving in *Stella* a personification of some divine conception, or some conception of the divine, in the mind of the poet. What that conception was we may partly guess from passages in Sidney's Defence of Poetry, where he refers to *Songs* and *Sonnets* (the first expression in the sense of Psalms) in these words: "Other sorts of Poetry, almost have we none, but that Lyrical kind of Songs and Sonnets, which, if the Lord gave us so good minds, how well it might be employed we all know, and with how heavenly fruits, both private and public, in singing the praises of the Immortal Beauty, the Immortal Goodness of that God who giveth us hands to write, and wits to conceive, of which we might well want words, but never matter; of which we could turn our eyes to nothing but we should ever find new budding occasions."

In another place of the Defence, Sidney refers to David as a poet in these words: "For what else is the awakening of his musical instrument; the often and free changing of persons; his notable prosopopœias, when he maketh you, as it were, see God coming in his majesty; his telling of the beasts' joyfulness, and hills leaping, but a heavenly poetry; wherein almost, he showeth himself a passionate *lover of that unspeakable and everlasting Beauty*, to be seen by the eyes of the mind, cleansed by faith."

Whoever reads Sidney's Sonnets, with these passages from his Defence of Poetry in mind, will surely see, in Stella, Sidney's *idea* of the Divine Beauty, or that which Plato—and Sidney was a Platonist—calls the Beautiful; not as applicable to a beautiful person or thing, but to the principle of Beauty; in one word, Plato means by it, the DIVINE.

We have no disposition to enter here upon the old discussion about the real and the ideal, the idea and the imagination, the one and the many, Plato disposing of the problem (as in the Philebus) by uniting the two expressions into one, and then discussing what he calls the one-and-many, which however, to the imagination, only adds one more to that which was already many; yet here also the single idea is recognized, comprehending in unity the one-and-many, just as it had comprehended the many before; showing, in fact, that there is no eluding the true constitution of the mind by the structure of language, which is not the master but the servant of the soul. It may domineer at first over the young and the immature, but in the end, that which was first must become the last; as our poet tells us in the 85th Sonnet, where he declares that, whatever may be said by others in the praise of the object address-ed, the object of his own passion, he could add some-thing more; but that addition, he tells us, was in his *thought*, which, he says, "though words come hind-most, holds his rank before."

It may aid a student of the beautiful in Art, to give the Phædrus a careful reading; for that dia-logue came from the country, and the time, where and when a sense of the Beautiful was exalted into religion.

Because Poets, and Philosophers also, have not un-frequently addressed this divine *something* as a mas-culine person, particular instances of it, as in the case of the Sonnets before us, have been explained by an appeal to a supposed custom, by which friends are said to have addressed each other in the language of love; not seeing that this only explains one ano-maly by an appeal to a greater; for the question recurs, What is the meaning of that love-literature of the Middle Ages? Abused, as it no doubt was, fully justifying Cervantes, still, the truth remains, that in the hands of the adepts, Dante, Petrarch, and others, Love was the synonym for Religion:

and this is the explanation of the fact that multitudes of the romances of the Middle Ages represent the hero of the story as falling in love at a Church— the church figuring the virgin-mother of the faith derived from it. Nothing is more common than the use of this expression, the mother, as applied to a church, and this is also a virgin-mother. In like manner, all places of education are mothers, it being the custom of all collegiate scholars to speak of what they call their Alma Mater. The analogous use of language led our poet, in the 3d Sonnet, to speak of a mother as applied to a subject of art; and, again, in the 16th Sonnet, he uses the expression "maiden gardens," meaning virgin or unwrought subjects; which, he means to say in that Sonnet, were open to the artist.

CHAPTER II.

ASKING the reader to bear in mind the extracts from Drayton and Sidney, we will proceed to show that the object addressed in the Shakespeare Sonnets is analogous to what the latter calls Immortal Beauty and Immortal Goodness, only suggesting, as a precaution, that these are not to be regarded under any form of the imagination, but conceived as spiritual.

That this may be done, no one need be told who is in the habit of prayer himself, or in the habit of attending prayer in the church; for to whom or what does the preacher address himself when, with eyes uplifted or closed, he approaches what he calls the throne of grace? Certainly the object addressed in such cases is no visible or imaginary form whatever, but a conceived spirit, the spirit revealed in religion, according to the declaration of the gospel—

"God is a spirit, and they that worship him must worship him in spirit and in truth."

The Beauty of this spirit is addressed by our poet in the first Sonnet under a figurative expression—
"Beauty's Rose:"

> From fairest creatures we desire increase,
> That thereby Beauty's Rose might never die,
> But as the riper should by time decease,
> His tender *heir* might bear his memory.

In this Sonnet the poet addresses the Spirit of Beauty, or the Beautiful, as the fountain of art; and, as proceeding from an artistic poet, the lines are an invocation to the Spirit of Beauty to become, as it were, his mistress, or, in the Helenic sense, his Muse or Inspiration, in order that he might perpetuate his sense of beauty in some adequate poetic form, which, preserving the figure, he calls an HEIR, precisely in the sense in which this word is used in the poet's dedication of Venus and Adonis to the Earl of Southampton, in which that poem is called the first *heir* of his invention.

This poetic *heir* is the child, the son, &c., so often referred to in most of the first sixteen or eighteen Sonnets of the series of one hundred and fifty-four, as published in the modern editions of Shakespeare's works.

We do not consider that the Sonnets, in their present order, were written throughout under one rigid idea, incapable of variation, or that they were written in the precise order in which we now have them. We admit, also, that there may possibly be some, now embraced in the series, which the writer of them might have excluded or modified, if the collection, when first made, had been under his control; and we have but little doubt that the collection, as it comes to us, may be wanting in some few Sonnets which may be found elsewhere, or may have been lost altogether. We also suppose that the Sonnets were written at various periods or stages of life, some of them in early life, when the ideal stood before the poet's mind in all its power, and others at a later period, when the vision had either partially left or threatened to leave him, or had undergone some transformations, though without ever being absolutely denied. We can believe that the poet ultimately outgrew, not the ideal itself, but some of the forms in which it had presented itself to his early imagination; and finally, we think we see where the poet probably ceased to indulge his imaginative faculty in the pure or abstract ideal, and confined himself to the more sober realities of practical life, though with improved powers of understanding the great world, which, assuredly, is but a fragment of life, when its unseen counterpart is not recognized and acknowledged.

In the first Sonnet the poet expresses a desire that Beauty's Rose might never die; but that as the riper should decease, his tender heir might bear his memory.

The meaning of this is, that the *forms* in which the beautiful has been expressed in former ages, are liable to become antiquated, insomuch as measurably to lose the power of expressing the beautiful. This is figured by their " decease; " and the poet's desire is, that he might be so endowed himself as to be able to take up the theme in some new form to keep alive the " memory " of it.

In the 108th Sonnet the poet himself refers to the classics of antiquity as being included among the class of writings subject to *decease* in the sense here stated; for, as we may observe in that Sonnet, the poet saw, in those classic works,

> the first conceit of love there bred, ·
> Where time and outward form would show it dead.

Not that Beauty itself can ever die, for this the poet tells us (Sonnet 18) has an "eternal summer;" but that in the progress of ages, owing to the mutability of language, its forms of expression become so antiquated that we may speak of them as dead: and yet it is one of the precious fruits of this study, that the adept is enabled to recognize the traces of the spirit wherever it has appeared in the world.

That the opening Sonnets are to be understood as invocations to the higher spirit of Beauty, or of life, may appear, in part, from the 78th Sonnet, where the *object*, figured as Beauty's Rose in the 1st Sonnet, is thus addressed:

> 78. So oft have I invoked THEE for my muse,
>   And found such fair assistance in my verse ; etc.

and the Sonnet concludes with these lines:

> Yet be most proud of that which I compile,
> Whose influence is thine and BORN of thee:
> In others' works thou dost but mend the style,
> And arts with thy sweet graces graced be ;
> But thou art all my art, and dost advance
> As high as learning my rude ignorance.

It is plain here, though we shall soon make it
more so, that the poet's Sonnets, the verses which he
"compiles," are the fruit, the very *born* of that
which, in the 1st Sonnet, is figured as Beauty's
Rose; and the reader is expected to see, in the
course of the explanation we have undertaken, that
this is the Spirit of Beauty, or the Beautiful in the
Platonic sense; and this spirit is in perfect harmony with the spirit of nature. Hence we may
here, in this 78th Sonnet, have a glimpse of the sense
in which Shakespeare may be regarded as himself
nature's child. He has often been so called, because he drew his inspiration from nature, this
being, as he says, all his art; or, to use his own
expression in Hamlet, he, of all men who ever wrote,
was enabled " to hold the mirror up to nature."

There may be more, but there are certainly two
species of poetry; and it is necessary to show that
our poet, while he knew that he was in possession of the subordinate form, as the result of education and a certain imitative power, desired to become the medium for the expression of that higher
form of poetry which is the direct result of the spirit
of life becoming active in the soul, under the power
of which the poet becomes impersonal: and here we

see one of the peculiar characteristics of Shakespeare, as seen in his dramas; or, rather, one of his
characteristics is, that he is not seen at all in his
writings as *a* man, but as life—the very object
addressed in the opening Sonnets.

The principle here stated, that nature, seen in
her spirit as life, is "all the art" of the poet, will
appear in several of the Sonnets; but, for the present, it will suffice to point to the 16th, in which
the poet seems to beseech the *spirit* to take a
"mightier way to make war upon the bloody tyrant
time," than to depend upon what he calls the *barren
rhyme* of his *pupil pen,*—meaning the results of his
mere imitative power—by becoming, itself, his immediate muse or inspiration; adding,

> To give away yourself keeps yourself still;
> And you must live, drawn by your own sweet skill.

This sweet skill is no other than nature's skill;
for nature always works divinely and sweetly. We
may make it appear otherwise when we undertake,
following a blind or perverse will, to work in contra-
vention of the divine laws as expressed in nature.

We are now prepared to show more directly how

the spirit is regarded by the poet of the Sonnets, for which purpose we appeal first to the 39th Sonnet, in which the *object*, or Beauty's Rose, is addressed as the better part of the poet himself, meaning undoubtedly the spirit of life,—the poet contemplating himself as having a double nature, which, for convenience, we may for the present define as natural and spiritual.

> 39 O how *thy* worth with manners may I sing,
>   When *thou* art all the better part of me ; etc.

If this does not appear plain, it may become so by turning to the 74th Sonnet, where we see that the poet speaks of consecrating his own better part to the *object* addressed, which, we must recollect, is figured as Beauty's Rose; and then he tells us that this better part is his own spirit:

> 74. My spirit is *thine*, the better part of me.

If the reader will scan these two Sonnets closely, the 39th and the 74th, he will see, as it were, the two spirits, the inner and the outer, regarded by the poet as ONE ; and here the reader may discover the principal secret of the Sonnets. This unity is the "precious one," which the poet tells us in the 22d Sonnet he will be as chary of as a tender nurse of its babe. In its beginning it is a babe, the new birth of genius, and no less the blessed child of faith, or faith itself, the one thing needful, as seen in the field of art; for although the poet is filled with a religious spirit, we must regard him as treating of Art, which, in his age, he tells us, in Sonnet 66, was "tongue-tied by authority; "—and here we may discover a hint of the reasons inducing the poet to use the hermetic form of writing.

But there is something which disturbs the poet's vision of the unity, and operates as a separation, between himself and his "better part.". By turning to the 44th Sonnet we shall see, beyond a doubt, that this disturbing element is no other than material nature, called "the dull substance of the flesh." This is that which troubled the poet, and gave occasion for that "sour leisure," which nevertheless gave him "sweet leave to entertain the time with thoughts of love," meaning divine love; and yet, this fleshly obstacle was a great grief to the poet: "Ah!" says he, "thought kills me, that I am not thought." His vision of the spirit was so

2

delightful and absorbing that, like Plotinus of old, he could not bear the *thought* of the interposed body, or flesh, which, in the 36th Sonnet, is referred to as the separable (or separating) *spite*, by which he was compelled to feel as if " removed " from the spirit—in which state his only consolation was, as just stated, from the 39th Sonnet, to entertain sweet thoughts of love, that is, of the spirit, the spirit of beauty.

We may find some confirmation of this view in the beautiful scene between Lorenzo and Jessica:

> How sweet the moonlight sleeps upon this bank !
> Here we will sit, and let the sounds of music
> Creep in our ears : soft stillness, and the night,
> Become the touches of sweet harmony.
> Sit, Jessica : look, how the floor of heaven
> Is thick inlaid with patterns of bright gold ;
> There's not the smallest orb, which thou behold'st,
> But in his motion like an angel sings,
> Still quiring to the young-eyed cherubins :
> Such harmony is in immortal souls ;
> But, whilst this muddy vesture of decay
> Doth grossly close it in, we cannot hear it.
>
> *Mer. of Ven.*

This " muddy vesture of decay," this " dull sub-

stance of the flesh," is referred to in the 20th Sonnet
as the "addition" to the otherwise feminine nature,
which in that Sonnet is seen as double, and is called
the master-mistress of the poet's passion—this being
a mystical expression for the object addressed in the
1st Sonnet as Beauty's Rose. The poet desires (in
the 20th Sonnet) to come into immediate relations
with the Spirit of Nature; but Nature, as visible, is,
in this Sonnet, called an "addition," meaning an addition to the Spirit of Beauty (or of Nature—for they
are one), and becomes obstructive. It is a hin-
drance to the poet's "purpose;" and the poet says,
substantially, addressing the Spirit,—Since Nature
has "prick'd" or decked thee out for the *affections*
to be exercised upon, called "woman's pleasure,"
give me, says he, thy pure or intellectual love, and
the "use" I will make of it shall also be for the
pleasure of the affections:—and we see he has done
this in both his Sonnets and his dramas, which may
be said to be addressed to that portion of man
which is often called the woman or feminine side of
man, meaning the affections; the Spirit indeed being
in them, but unseen except to the Spirit, or to those
who have what the poet calls "lover's eyes" (Sonnets 23, 55).

CHAPTER III.

WE might stop here, satisfied that enough has been disclosed to convince any candid student, and enable him to proceed by himself in searching out the arcane beauties of these wonderful Sonnets; but as we have undertaken to put a face upon them which, it is believed, is quite if not altogether unknown in this age, we will proceed to point out the meaning of some of the Sonnets, which are liable to be misunderstood by those who are unacquainted with hermetic writings.

Beauty's Rose, recognized as life, is seen by the poet as the spirit of humanity; and because this is viewed as having no direct relation to time, the poet sees it both in the past and in the future. Thus, in Sonnet 59, the poet casts his eye backward, so to speak, desiring to see the image of his idea in some " antique book," five hundred years old, in order that he might

see what the "old world" had said of the greatest
wonder of the world, MAN; that he might judge
whether we, of modern times, are mended, or whether man in former times was the better.

In the 106th Sonnet we may see that the poet's
wish was at least partially accomplished; for he saw
the purpose of the class of books known as tales or
romances of chivalry, containing the "praise of
ladies dead, and lovely knights." He saw that their
purpose was a mystical one, and that it was, in fact,
to express "such a beauty" as was then before the
poet's eyes. Referring to the romancers, he says:

106. I see their antique pen would have expressed
    Even such a Beauty as you [addressing Beauty's Rose] mas-
      ter now.
  So all their praises are but prophecies
    Of this our time, all you prefiguring;
  And, for they looked but with divining eyes,
    They had not skill enough your praise to sing :
  For we, which now behold these present days,
  Have eyes to wonder, but lack tongues to praise.

But whilst we see the poet, in the 59th and 106th
Sonnets, casting his longing eyes backward in time,
to discover what the old world had said of the
miracle then under his own eye, we may see him, in

the 32d Sonnet, looking forward inquiringly, anxious
in regard to the point, as to how his own work in
art-writing was likely to be viewed.

32. It thou

[says he, addressing the spirit of humanity, his own
" better part," seen as the spirit of life] :

> If thou survive my well-contented day,
>   When that churl death with dust my bones shall cover,
> And shalt by fortune once more re-survey
>   These poor rude lines of thy deceased lover,
> Compare them with the bettering of the time ; etc.

These lines are addressed to any modern reader
who recognizes the spirit of the poet, by sharing it ;
and the poet asks, of such a reader, that he will
judge of the poet's verses with a due consideration
of the improvements of knowledge, &c., which he
calls the " bettering of the time "—evidently antici-
pating a progress in knowledge ; and then he proceeds, referring to his own verses :

> And though they be outstripp'd by every pen,
> Preserve them for my love, not for their rhyme,
>   Exceeded by the height of happier men.
> O then

[he continues, as if addressing us in this so-called enlightened century],

> O then vouchsafe me but this loving thought!
>   Had my friend's Muse grown with this growing age,
> A dearer birth

[the reader should mark this expression—a dearer *birth*, the very son invoked in the first sixteen or eighteen Sonnets—]

> A dearer birth than this his love had brought,
>   To march in ranks of better equipage :
> But since he died, and poets better prove,
> Theirs for their style I'll read, his for his love.

It is scarcely possible for an adult reader to mistake the meaning of this Sonnet, which, with the 59th and the 106th, shows us the poet in the act of casting his eyes both backward and forward for ages, to catch a glimpse of the view which might have been entertained in the past, or was likely to be in the then future, of the *object* before his own clear vision under the figure of Beauty's Rose.

If we are not mistaken in the meaning of these Sonnets, the 32d, 59th, and 106th, then the ordinary method of interpreting the Sonnets, as addressed to a person, contemporary with the poet, must not only be abandoned, but we must conclude that the *object* addressed is something conceived to be as permanent in life as life itself.

That this is the true point of view will appear from many of the Sonnets, but particularly from the 83d, in which the object is addressed as " extant " (in the 84th as an "example"), in the sense of being an exemplar, by which to judge of what has been said of it in ancient times, compared with the power of a " modern quill " to represent it.

Thus far the view we have presented is simple and natural, and hardly admits of being questioned. There is nothing strained or forced in this interpretation, while, on the supposition of a *person* as the object addressed in the Sonnets, the student is perpetually embarrassed with inexplicable difficulties.

But the reader must not expect to enter easily into this field of study. The Sonnets are full of mysteries, and need the closest attention for their comprehension; but with patient thought on his own part, the student may gradually feel that he is being drawn into something like an acquaintance with the mode of thinking of the most wonderful mind that has ever appeared in literature; for, in the Sonnets before us, we may discover what may be called the principles of thought in Shakespeare.

Many have supposed that in the Sonnets we are to find some account of the outward life of the poet · but it is not so much his outward as his inward life that is in some degree to be understood from those starlike manifestations of his spiritual nature.

Students of the Sonnets have supposed them addressed to more than one person; that, while the earlier portion are addressed to some man, at all events, whether to the Earl of Southampton or not, the latter portion must have been addressed, they think, to one or more women, and certainly, as they imagine, to some one of no very reputable character.

To clear up some of these points, let the reader consider that the object addressed, although conceived as a unity, or perhaps we should say a perfect harmony, as may be seen in many of the Sonnets, particularly in the 105th and 108th, is nevertheless of a composite nature (though not in a mechanical sense), as designated in the 20th Sonnet, where Beauty's Rose is called the master-mistress of the poet's passion, that is, of his love. We have already intimated that for convenience this double nature may be regarded as soul and body—not that by the mere use of words the nature of these expressions can be understood.

The dramatic writings of the poet will show some illustrations of this point. Thus King Richard, in the dungeon at Pomfret, soliloquizes :

> I have been studying how I may compare
> This prison, where I live, to the world;
> And for because the world is populous,
> And here is not any creature but myself,
> I cannot do it: but I'll hammer it out.
> My brain I'll prove the female to my soul;
> My soul, the father: and these two beget
> A generation of still breeding thoughts,
> And these same thoughts people this same little world;
> In humors like to the people of this world;
> For no thought is contented.

If in this soliloquy we change the expression *brain*, and compare the body to the female, we shall be even nearer the truth, and be in a better position for a comprehension of the Sonnets under a still broader theory of soul, body, and spirit, three in one.

It would be easy to point out other parallels to the Sonnets in other portions of the soliloquy,—for example, the allusion to music, as compared with the 8th Sonnet,—the soul itself being a musical instrument, though it may require a David to awaken it into expression. But we will not go too much into detail.

In the soliloquy of Richard, the soul, we see, is compared to a father, and the brain to a mother; yet the two are one in the poet, who may be imagined as addressing that same soul in the opening Sonnets, supposed by many to have been some person, and generally believed to have been the Earl of Southampton.

In the Prologue to Henry the Fifth there is a passage which may very well be here considered, as it serves to show how the poet conceived the unity of man as expressing at the same time the many :—" into a thousand parts," says he, "divide one man, and make imaginary puissance,"—as if by this process the individual could, as it were, bring into his presence the entire drama, and all its *personæ.*

In the 1st Sonnet the object addressed is figured as Beauty's Rose; but in the 20th the double nature appears, and Beauty's Rose is

called the master-mistress of the poet's love.
This view presents no difficulty, for the object,
though double, is still a unity; but in this unity
the student must perceive on the one side (the
feminine side), a sufficient provision for an endless generation of " still breeding thoughts ;"
while on the masculine or soul side, so to say,
there is no division conceivable ; and this is the
characteristic of what some call the pure reason;
for this is always one and the same: we do not
say this of reasoning, but of reason. Let the
reader catch the poet's idea in the drama, and
then see how it is expressed in the abstract Sonnets, particularly in the 144th and 147th Sonnets.
The 144th commences—

144.   Two loves

[or tendencies, the poet means to say, precisely in
the sense of St. Paul in the 7th chapter of Romans]

> Two loves I have of comfort and despair,
>> Which like two spirits do suggest me still ;

[that is, the two loves or tendencies drew or
instigated the poet in contrary directions : he pro-
ceeds] :

> The better angel or [tendency] is a MAN right fair,
>   The worser spirit a woman, color'd ill.

In the 11th line of the Sonnet the poet tells us that both of the spirits were "from,"—that is, they proceeded from himself; or, in other words, they were in himself: and, to be brief, these two spirits are no other than those popularly known as the reason and the affections, the latter being the feminine side of the master-mistress; and here we must see the Eve or evil side of Adam, wherein corruption becomes possible, when the affections pass into passions in a bad sense. This is the meaning of the expression *color'd ill*, color being a figurative word for the changeable passions.

We do not look in the direction of the passions for truth and reason; and although the reason in itself is incorruptible, yet, in the composite nature of man, the man himself, when under the dominion of the passions, comes under a cloud ; and then, in the way of a metonym, the reason is said to be clouded or corrupted.

This view will fully prepare the reader for the 147th Sonnet, to wit :

147.   My love

[here regarded as the passion side of life]

> My love is as a fever, longing still
>   For that which longer nurseth the disease;
> Feeding on that which doth preserve the ill,
>   The uncertain sickly appetite to please ;
> My *reason*, the physician to my love,
>   Angry that his prescriptions are not kept,
> Hath left me, etc.

Here the *reason* and the *love* are the man and the woman of the 144th Sonnet, the former being the physician, who is said to have left the poet : that is, as expressed in the 144th Sonnet, the female evil had tempted his better angel until he is said to have left his side.

CHAPTER IV.

AT this stage of the development exhibited in the Sonnets, the poet had become deeply sensible of the evil nature of the affections when, refusing obedience to reason, they degenerate into passions; though, at the first, they had not appeared so, but had worn an angel-like face, which the poet had thought both "fair and bright." Hence the closing lines of the 147th Sonnet:

> I have sworn thee fair, and thought thee bright,
> Who art as black as hell, as dark as night.

We have already taken one or two confirmations of these views from the poet's dramas, and will here take one from the closing scene of the 2d Act of Cymbeline, where the poet has evidently framed a scene as if on purpose to place a character

in a suitable dramatic position for an appropriate
expression of the doctrine just indicated, in which
the evil side of life is placed to the feminine ac
count.

Posthumous is artistically placed in a position
to doubt the fidelity of Imogen, and then ex
claims :

> * * * Could I find out
> The woman's part in me ! For there's no motion
> That tends to vice in man, but I affirm
> It is the woman's part : be it lying, note it,
> The woman's ; flattering, hers ; deceiving, hers ;
> Lust and rank thoughts, hers, hers ; revenges, hers ;
> Ambitions, covetings, change of prides, disdain,
> Nice longings, slanders, mutability,
> All faults that may be named, nay that hell knows,
> Why, hers, in part, or all ; but rather all ;
> For even to vice
> They are not constant, but are changing still
> One vice, but of a minute old, for one
> Not half so old as that. I'll write against them,
> Detest them, curse them,—Yet 'tis greater skill,
> In a true hate, to pray they have their will :
> The very devils cannot plague them better.

If the poet is to be condemned for thus figuring
the evil side of life by charging it upon woman, it

must be recollected that he has an ancient and a
high authority for it in Genesis. On the other
hand, all writers, ancient and modern, have united
in setting truth before us under the image of a
virgin, usually described as a king's daughter, and
thus called a princess, always described as a sur-
passing beauty,

> Which steals men's eyes, and women's souls amazeth.

We understand very well that the poet does not
apply all this denunciation to " lovely woman," but
to what he calls the woman's part in man; and so
far as there is any truth in it at all it is as applicable
to what may as appropriately be called the woman's
part in woman; for the double nature of the master-
mistress is shared by both man and woman, these
expressions signifying, in the Sonnets, the reason and
the affections. Hence, in several of the Sonnets, the
two natures are referred to as separate persons; as
in the 42d and also in the 133d and 134th Sonnets,
the poet himself making a third person in the unity,
in some cases even a fourth; for the unity always remains, no matter how many of the composite elements are referred to.

The 133d and 134th Sonnets are extremely

complicated, but they are to be explained upon the
theory we have assumed. To understand the 133d
Sonnet, we must consider that the poet has been
reflecting upon the *pain* which his own misconduct
has brought upon his better nature, as if this "better
part" of himself was separated from him (Sonnet
36) ; and he condemns that (woman's part) in him
which has misled him. Hence he exclaims, line 1,
as we will paraphrase it,—Beshrew that heart (or
affection in me) which has misled me, and induced
the pain I feel from the thought of having wounded
the higher spirit, as well as me ; proceeding, line 3:
—is it not enough that I should suffer alone, for
what I have done, but must my better spirit be
brought into slavery, or suffering, in addition to my
own pain? and he continues, line 5 : that cruel
affection (human) has made a division in my own
nature, separating me from "my most true mind"
(as expressed in the 113th Sonnet), and hast made
my *better part* suffer even more than me; thus dis-
uniting my whole self, leaving me in utter desola-
tion; or, as in line 7, "utterly forsaken : " and now
he prays, line 9, that his better self would take his
(human) heart into its own steel (or strong) bosom
(or nature) :—where he proposes to "bond" himself

for the release (from suffering) of his higher self;
and will constitute himself a guard for the faithful
execution of the bond.   This being all (metaphy-
sically) arranged, he says, line 12, addressing his
" better part,"—Thou can'st not be rigorous with me,
thus imprisoned in thy steel bosom, because I,
being *pent* in thee, am thine [or thee].   "Yet thou
wilt be so "—because, as we explain it, notwith-
standing all this wrestling with the spirit, he could
not free himself from a sense of his demerits; as
appears also in the 134th Sonnet.

The expression in the 13th line, " being *pent* in
thee," carries us to the poet's sense of the unity, just
as, in the last line of the 135th Sonnet, the language
" think all but (or only) one," is a clear indication
of the same doctrine.

This may appear to be an overstrained solution
of the mysticism in these Sonnets, but a careful consideration of the poet's doctrine of the duality and
triplicity, all in the unity, as seen in the 42d Sonnet, will reconcile the difficulties.   In the Sonnet
just named, the poet declares: " My friend and I
are one," the *friend* being the object addressed,
called the better part of himself in the 39th Sonnet.

That this *object* was not a merely contemporary

person, will become more and more apparent as the reader becomes familiar with the idea, that the poet is addressing what Emerson charmingly calls the Over-Soul. Thus, the 53d Sonnet is surely address-ed to the Source of all being :

> 53. What is your substance, whereof are you made,
>   That millions of strange shadows on you tend ?
>   Since every one hath, every one, one shade,
>   And you, but one, can every shadow lend.
>   Describe Adonis, and the counterfeit
>   Is poorly imitated after you ;
>   On Helen's cheek all art of beauty set,
>   And you in Grecian tires are painted new :
>   Speak of the spring, and foizon * of the year ;
>   The one doth shadow of your beauty show,
>   The other as your bounty doth appear,
>   And you in every blessed shape we know.
>   In all external grace you have some part,
>   But you like none, none you, for constant heart.

This Sonnet clearly recognizes the constancy or permanence of the spirit in variable nature. It may remind us somewhat of the maya doctrine of the Hindoos, as it also reminds us of the doctrine of· those who would have us see God in all things, or all things in God.

* Plenty, or harvest.

As between Jacobi and Goethe, our poet would undoubtedly have sided with the latter, who declared that nature reveals God, while Jacobi was of opinion that nature conceals God.

To those who do not perceive God in nature, the latter must wear a "black," terrible aspect, to be likened only to death; but to our poet this material existence was illumined by the spirit,

> 27. Which, like a jewel hung in ghastly night,
>   Makes black night beauteous and her old face new.

If the reader still doubts as to the object addressed, let him turn to the 122d Sonnet, and study its meaning. The "gift," the "tables," referred to in the 1st line, are two expressions for one thing, the written law of Moses—often called the gift of God, said to have been written on tables of stone. St. Paul speaks, in the 3d chapter 2d Corinth., of tables in the same sense, and tells us of the law written upon the fleshly *tables* of the heart by the Spirit of God, which gave him life, and by which he was enabled to leave the written law—called Christ in the flesh—"behind," calling the same written law elsewhere a schoolmaster, who may be dismissed after his lesson has been taught. In like manner,

our poet tells us of the tables (or law) being full
charactered (or written) within his brain, where, he
was sure, it would remain " beyond all date, even to
eternity ; " or, at the least, so long as brain and
heart have faculty by nature to subsist; adding that,
until each be lost in oblivion, the true record of the
spirit upon the heart can never be missed : and then
he refers to the written law, as a " poor retention,"
unable to hold so much as the spiritual writing upon
the heart—in keeping with the true sense of the closing verse of the gospel of John : and then he says :

Nor need I tallies [or writings] thy dear love to score,—adding,
therefore, to give [the writings] from me was I bold ; [that is, he
left them *behind*] to trust [as he says], those tables [of the heart
and brain] which receive thee more ; and he concludes :

To keep an adjunct [an artificial reminder] to remember thee,
Were to import forgetfulness in me.

We do not see how this 122d Sonnet can have
any other meaning than the one here assigned to it ;
and if this is its true sense, then it discloses the
object addressed as clearly as figurative language
can do it, when used by a mystical writer.

It must be observed that, in making this and
other interpretations, the interpreter is not express-

ing his own individual opinions with regard to the divine law. He is merely showing how the poet felt related to it; but the reader should perceive that the poet by no means repudiates or denies the law. On the contrary, by implication, he fully sustains it, only saying, with St. Paul, that he found it written in his "brain and heart."

There is another and a very mystical allusion to the Mosaic law in the two concluding Sonnets of the series, both of which refer to the same mystery, which is, the mystery of the spirit in the letter. In the 153d Sonnet, *Cupid* signifies love, in a religious sense; the *maid of Dian* is a *virgin* truth of nature; the *cold valley-fountain* is the letter of the law—called a cold well in the 154th Sonnet: and truth, we all know, is said to be at the bottom of a well. In this cold valley-fountain Moses, by the aid of a genuine (a virgin) nature-truth, steeped love's brand, at a time when the world, not Cupid indeed, had fallen asleep with regard to religion. The letter is then said to have borrowed the holy fire of love (holding it like the fire in the bush—which was unconsumed, as is the letter- of the law); and the fire gave to the law of Moses, " a dateless lively heat still to endure," making it a " seething bath, which yet men prove against strange [spiritual] maladies a sovereign care."

153. But

[continues the poet]

> But at my mistress' eye love's brand new-fir'd;
>   The boy for trial needs would touch my breast;
> I sick withal, the help of bath desired,
>   And thither hied, a sad distemper'd guest,
> But found no cure; the bath for my help lies
> Where Cupid got new fire,—my mistress' eyes.

What, now, are the eyes of the mistress here referred to, but the reason and affections, which, when rightly understood, will disclose the true unity in their own harmony ; for the affections are so far from being evil in themselves, that they are truly divine.

The sickness of the poet, when touched by Cupid, signifies only the common experience, that whoever makes any progress in what is called spiritual life, discovers, by discovering a higher measure of truth, that his own previous life falls short of the true " stature of Christ," as St. Paul calls it, and he must needs feel heart-sick at the discovery if he still has in him the elements of improvement.

The poet was sick in that sense, and sought the help of the law; but found, upon trial, no benefit—because he had discovered already, as we have seen in the 122d Sonnet, the true law written upon the tablet of his heart. His recourse, then, was to turn more devotedly to the spiritual powers of the soul, the hermetic sun and moon, and endeavor rightly to understand them.

It was to accomplish this end that many of the Sonnets were written, for they are essentially soul-studies; and we venture to say that no one will truly understand them who does not study them from a religious stand-point.

The word love, as used in the Sonnets, must in the main be understood as religious love, in the sense of St. John, who tells us that God is love. The poet's soul was filled with it; and he saw that the universe was filled with it. In the 40th Sonnet we may see something of the truth of this remark:

> 40.   Take all my loves, my love, yea, take them all;
>   What hast thou then more than thou had'st before?
>   No love, my love, that thou may'st true love call;
>   All mine was thine, before thou had'st this more.

Here we see that no love can be truly called love

3

but the love of the object addressed in the Sonnets under the figure of Beauty's Rose; and it abundantly appears that that object was the higher spirit of life, the better part of the poet himself, before which the student may see the poet surrendering himself in the deepest sense of genuine humility, as in Sonnets 88, 89, and several others,—a humility, except before the supreme spirit of truth, which would be nearly below contempt. In our poet, however, this humility is perfectly consistent with a lofty exultation under a conscious sense of the immortality he foresaw must wait upon his labors,—as in Sonnets 55, 63, 65, 81, 107, and many others.

The poet's humility has nothing in it to humble him before man, but only before God; and this is truly the source of his perfect independence of the judgments of man, so strongly set forth in the 121st Sonnet. The perfect independence of the poet is shown also in the 123d Sonnet. There are no men so truly independent as those who live in the fear of God, and walk humbly before him.

In the 41st Sonnet we have shown the poet's sense of the unity as seen in *love*. In the 135th and 136th Sonnets the unity is seen in its *power*, under the symbol of the *will ;* for these Sonnets, far from

being a play upon the poet's name, as many suppose,
contain the poet's metaphysical view of God as
Power. His doctrine is, that the will, or the power
of God is supreme, and the poet's prayer is that his
own individual will might be included or taken up,
as it were, in the will or power of God. There is no
refinement in metaphysical disquisitions which can
surpass the mingled acuteness of thought and holy
aspiration exhibited in the two Sonnets, the 135th
and 136th. The poet is sure of the doctrine of om-
nipotence; but he feels, also, a sense of his individuality; and yet he sees that his own individuality
must be absorbed in the supreme. He is to think
"all but one, and himself in that one." From this
point of view these two Sonnets are very beautiful,
and truly religious; whereas, in the ordinary mode
of interpretation they are nothing but a ridiculous
play upon a word. We do not deny, however, but
that the poet had his eye upon his own name, but
only as a symbol of himself, and he saw himself in
his soul or life; and that he saw in the one life of
the universe. And thus, in part, at least, we may
see the doctrines of the poet in his dramas, where
fitting dramatic scenes make occasions for declara-
tions of them; as in Romeo and Juliet, the Capulet
thus addresses the Montague:

What 's Montague ? it is nor hand, nor foot,
Nor arm, nor face, nor any other part
Belonging to a man.   O ! be some other name.
    *   *   Romeo, doff thy name ;
And for thy name, which is no part of thee,
Take all myself.

We regard the Sonnets as containing the abstract
doctrines of the poet, developed under the most in-
tense contemplations of life; and that, in symbolic
form, the poet has enclosed in them what were to
him eternal principles.   In the dramas, these same
principles are expressed under images of time,
through imaginary persons and imaginary scenes.

Many will no doubt suppose that the language
. of Romeo, in the 1st Scene of the 1st Act, expresses
a merely local truth, where he says, of Juliet :

O she is rich in beauty; only poor,
That when she dies with beauty dies her store.

*   *   *   *   *   *   *   *   *   *

For beauty starv'd with her severity,
Cuts beauty off from all posterity.

Here is language similar to that of the opening
Sonnets, as addressed to Beauty's Rose, supposed to
be a young man, the Earl of Southampton; but in

truth, the figure in the Sonnets encloses the abstract eternal truth in the heaven of art; while, in the drama, the poet uses the ideal truth in the region of time. Truth, in itself, is one only; but it admits of infinite forms of expression in time. Thus love, in its truth, is but one, and St. John, in telling us that God is love, sufficiently defines love itself, by a mere conversion of the language.

But just here the "addition" (Sonnet 20) seems interposed to obstruct, as it were, the pure action of the spirit. This so-called "addition" takes many names in the course of the Sonnets, besides that of the "separable spite" (Sonnet 36), and several others already referred to. In Sonnet 137 this "addition" is "the bay where all men ride," as it is also "the wide world's common place" of the same Sonnet. This is the "painted beauty" of Sonnet 21 —simply nature, considered as visible merely, and not conceived in the spirit of beauty. It is that which "covers" the spirit (Sonnet 22). It is "beauty's form" of Sonnet 24, which had been "stelled" (or engraved) by the eye upon the poet's heart (or "bosom's shop"). It is the "ghastly night" of the 27th Sonnet, when not illumined by the spirit, or "jewel," so "precious" to the poet. It makes the

" base clouds " of the 33d Sonnet, sent with " ugly
rack " across the " celestial face " of the spirit, or it
is the " region cloud " (of the same Sonnet) " mask-
ing " the spirit from the mental sight of the poet.
While the poet attaches himself to the external, or
to things of time, he represents himself as " absent "
from the spirit, as in Sonnets 41, 97, 109, &c. The
" addition " is the " wardrobe " of the 52d Sonnet,
which is said to hide the " robe "—the robe here
figuring the spirit. This same " addition " is called,
in the 125th Sonnet, a " suborned informer," above
which the " true soul " is said to stand, absolutely
free from its control. In the 126th Sonnet it is
called by its usual name, simply nature, " sovereign
mistress over wrack; " and the poet sees that her
" quietus " is only to be secured by that sort of a
surrender of one's self which is implied in a perfect
obedience to its laws, wherein the spirit reigns.
But the student should be careful not to imagine he
fully conceives the *true subject* of the mystery under
any mere names, and should especially guard against
supposing that this so-called " addition " can be
understood through the eye alone, or through any
or all of the five senses, as set out in the 141st Sonnet; yet the 69th Sonnet was designed to teach that

even visible nature is perfect in its own simple truth, as likewise is the heart or inner life when accepted in its own true life, and is not "confounded" by attempting to look into its beauty by "guess," which only adds to the perfect "flower" "the rank smell of weeds."

CHAPTER V.

WE could proceed thus, and notice something
of a universal character in almost every Sonnet, but
might then deprive the student of the satisfaction of
making discoveries for himself.

The so-called " extern " of the 125th Sonnet is
another of the many references to the mere material
side of nature.   It is the " dull substance of the
flesh " of the 44th Sonnet.   This flesh it was, that
" canopied " the spirit within, but which benefited
the poet nothing; or, as expressed in the 20th Sonnet, it was " nothing to his purpose."   His desire
was to be " obsequious " in the heart, that is, the
essence, or spirit of life: and this he saw required
the self-denial of Scripture, demanding a complete
surrender of the " me," or self, for the spirit, as set
out also in the 126th Sonnet; for the truth of the
doctrine does not depend upon its having been de-

clared in an " antique book; " but its truth is recognized there, because it is now " extant " in the nature of things (sonnet 83).

In the 127th Sonnet " black " signifies *evil ;* and the poet means to say, that in the early age of the world, sometimes called the golden age, or the age of innocence, *evil* was not counted *good ;* and he means also to represent that the spirit of truth was in mourning over the degeneracy of his age, which is figured by the " black eyes " of his mistress ; and this simply signifies that the poet's own spirit mourned over the depravity of the times in which he lived.

There are many evidences in the Sonnets that the poet looked upon the age in which he lived as rude and "unbred;" (he means, uncultivated in art, this being his particular field.) Thus, in the 108th Sonnet, he evidently refers to classical " antiquity," where he saw "the first conceit of love;" and there he saw, Sonnet 104, what he calls the " summer " of Beauty, telling his own "unbred age," as he calls it, "Ere you were born, was *beauty's* summer dead."

Mystical writers have sometimes compared the mere physical " extern " of life to *wood*, fashioned

3*

by the spirit into infinite shapes; but this class
of writers despise nothing in nature, and therefore honor the material in which the spirit works.
This must serve as a hint for understanding the
128th Sonnet.

> 128. How oft, when thou, my Musick, musick play'st,
>   Upon that *blessed wood* whose motion sounds
>   With thy sweet fingers, &c.

In this Sonnet, as elsewhere, the poet shows his
desire to penetrate the essence of things, here wishing to " kiss the tender inward of the [spiritual]
hand " whose sweet touches bring all nature into
harmony, figured by music. Beauty's Rose is
here styled the poet's Musick, being the principle
of harmony, when in harmony itself.

The reader may or may not recognize a passage in the last scene of Cymbeline as having
some connection with the idea expressed in the
128th Sonnet. When the very involved and complicated events of that drama are finally brought
into clear day and perfect consistency, a sooth-
sayer is brought forward, who, speaking as an oracle,
declares that " the *fingers* of the powers above do
tune the harmony of this peace."

There appears to be some error, perhaps typographical, in the 129th Sonnet. If in the place of "till," in the second line, we read *in*, there will at least be some sense in that part of the Sonnet; whereas, as it now reads, we do not see what to make of it, and are willing to let it pass as incomprehensible.

The student of the Sonnets should not form in his mind a rigid *image* of the object addressed, but should conceive that object poetically through the mind of the poet himself as far as possible; and then he will have no difficulty in understanding such Sonnets as the 138th, which commences:

> 138. When my love swears that she is made of truth,
> I do believe her, though I know she lies.

Here the poet does not address a woman, as all the critics appear to think, thereupon making pointed inferences touching the poet's life; but he has in his mind an idea of the feminine side of the double object originally conceived as the master-mistress of his passion; and the purpose here is to show that however "bright" and "fair" the mere passion side of life may appear to be, it is not to

be trusted when separated from the masculine or
reason side of our rational nature.

We have already said that in the 144th Sonnet
the poet lets us see his double nature, the man and
the woman, his reason and his affections—the latter
as the passions.

In the 146th Sonnet, the poet concludes to sacri-
fice the passion side of the master-mistress, the
body being called, in the 1st line, sinful earth; in
the 4th line, outward walls; in the 6th line, fading
mansion; and in the 9th line, the servant. The
arraigning powers (2d line) are of course the passions, by which the poet had been misled. These
are the fallen angels; for, as already stated, the
passions in their own nature are not evil, and it is a
mistake to teach that they are so.

But now the poet resolves (the same 146th
Sonnet) to "buy terms divine, by selling hours
of dross;" that is, he determines to surrender the
temporal for the eternal; and this he calls "feeding
on death, which feeds on men;" and he concludes
that, death being dead, there will be no more
dying then.

In the 147th Sonnet the feminine side of the
poet's nature is called love, and is compared to a

fever. Reason, the man of the 144th Sonnet, as already intimated, is the physician (5th line), whose "prescriptions" are said not to have been followed, and therefore it is that the poet finds himself abandoned by his reason: and now he sees clearly, that the affections, when not under the control of reason, are "as black as hell," though they had not appeared so in the glory of his first idea, in which they were full of feminine grace.

Here it is that the poet feels the need of what, in the 153d Sonnet, he calls a "seething bath." In one word, in his affliction, he looks toward those external ceremonies or writings where the world, for the most part, finds relief in spiritual troubles and trials. But here, as we have seen, he found no relief, for he had himself touched the very foundations of them, as he shows in Sonnet 122.

In several of the closing Sonnets, from about the 127th, we must consider the poet as in a transitional state. He is in a suffering condition, and is uncertain, for a time, whether to look for relief to his *ideal*, or to the "cold valley-fountain" (Sonnet 153).

The tendency of the poet to a transitional state is shown in the 102d Sonnet, where he says:

> Our love was new, and then but in the spring,
>
> When I was wont to greet it with my lays;
>
> As Philomel in summer's front doth sing,
>
> And stops her pipe in growth of riper days, &c.

Shelley's Ode to Intellectual Beauty may throw some light upon the state of mind of our poet as manifested in several of the closing Sonnets of the series, for Shelley too, like our poet, had looked on "nature's naked loveliness," and not without some of the consequences of that vision (vide his Adonais).

In the 148th Sonnet the self-complainings continue.

In the 149th the sufferer assents to the justice of God, though somewhat in a querulous mood. The sufferer's faith is supreme in the midst of his trials; but it is plain, from this Sonnet, that whilst he could not clearly see the justice (or love) in his afflictions, he, like Job of old, would not relinquish his faith or trust, but preferred to consider himself "blind," admitting that there were those who could comprehend the mystery of evil in life. Those that can (says he), that is, those who are able, "see thou lov'st," but for himself, he acknowledges himself "blind."

In the 150th Sonnet the poet wonders at the

power of the unseen spirit over him.   To understand
this Sonnet, the student (for we do not address the
mere careless everyday reader) may do well to consider, that the object of the poet's contemplations is
described, in the 27th Sonnet, as a "jewel, hung in
ghastly night;" in the 24th Sonnet, as a "picture,"
hanging in the poet's "bosom's shop;" in Sonnet
22, its beauty is said to be but "the seemly raiment
of the poet's heart;" in Sonnet 43, it is seen in con-
templation (as in a dream), "as shining brightly
dark, and darkly bright;" or, as he might have
said, it is seen here as through a glass darkly.   In
the 31st Sonnet, it is "the grave where buried love
doth live,"—the very thought of which, in Sonnet
30, ends all sorrows, and restores all losses—almost
the language of Isaiah and Jeremiah.   In the 67th
Sonnet the poet exclaims, "Ah! why with infection must *he* live,"—referring to (his) presence in
the flesh, which is subject to corruption; but in
Sonnets 95 and 96 we see that the presence of the
spirit beautifies its tabernacle, covering every blot,
and turning all things to fair which eyes can see.
This does not arise from its mere presence, for it is
omnipresent ; but it proceeds from the soul's recog-
nition of it.

In view of these allusions—and there are many others similarly illustrative—let the student translate, as we may say, the 150th Sonnet, and he may see that the poet had his spiritual eye upon a divine principle, which has the power to make "ill things appear becoming," and whose presence is such a manifestation of "skill" (or wisdom) that the very refuse of its works exceeds in worth all that is commonly called good in life. But the chief wonder is, that a sense of this marvellous thing makes its possessor love what others "abhor," including, of course, death itself; and the poet considers that, as he has so passed to what the Scripture calls "the other side," as to fall in love with what the world calls "unworthiness," he might, on that account, hope to be received into favor.

The expression, "thy unworthiness," will doubtless be a stumbling-block to many. It is not that the poet sees any real unworthiness in the object addressed as Beauty's Rose. But that object is double, as we see in the 20th Sonnet, and from this it comes that, in contemplating either portion by itself, there are apparent defects; as, to be plain, the soul, regarding the material side alone, sees what is called unworthiness; but this not only disappears

when seen in the spirit, but there is then seen a
certain "skill" (or wisdom) in those apparent defects which compels the love of the poet; for the
presence of the spirit "turns all things to fair that
eyes can see," Sonnet 95.

We can proceed no further in this direction; but
must leave the reader to determine the sense of these
mysterious allusions, the discovery of which may
make him reconciled "to look even upon sin and
crime, not as hinderances, but to honor and love
them as furtherances of what is holy,"—which is
said to be the last step in the Christian's life.

There are still a few other Sonnets which may be
separately noticed, trying the patience, it may be,
of those who feel sufficiently acquainted with the
whole series; but this class of readers may consider
that an attempt of this kind must necessarily be ad
dressed to all classes of readers, some of whom may
be entirely unacquainted with what is called hermetic "learning."

The Sonnets, we say, belong to the class of hermetic writings. They carry one sense to the eye
and the ear, but have another ("ensconced" in
them, Sonnet 49) for the head and the heart. That

the Sonnets belong to this species of writing may be
made sufficiently apparent even by expressions and
allusions in the Sonnets themselves.

The designation of the object addressed, in the
20th Sonnet, as the master-mistress of the poet's
passion, is mystical, and has no literal sense whatever. The last two Sonnets in the series, the 153d
and 154th, are so utterly destitute of literal sense,
that some editors have considered them as out of
place with the Sonnets, and discreditable to Shakespeare; though to an eye practiced in hermetic
writings they are full of meaning, and are known to
be of the highest importance to the collection—even
a sort of key to the whole; for, when understood,
they show that the poet developed under a perfect
freedom from all the trammels of traditional conven-
tionalisms.

In the 52d Sonnet the poet feels that he is in
possession of a certain "key," which opens to him a
"sweet up-locked treasure." This is the secret key
of the spirit, the very secret of the Lord, which,
though disclosed or revealed in the Scripture, is only
disclosed or made known under certain conditions.
We will not dwell upon this solemn and sacred
mystery, and will only remark that this mysterious

key is not acquired from books solely, but from a
true life.   In its acquisition books are only instru-
mental, and truly accomplish nothing, except under
the blessing of God.

In the 75th Sonnet we may see the spirit referred
to as serving, for the poet's thoughts, " as food for
life,"—for the security of which the poet holds such
strife, he tells us, " as 'twixt a miser and his wealth
is found."   Now he " counts it best to be with his
treasure alone ; " that is, he considers it best to hold
his secret hermetically in his own bosom, or, to use
the language of Sonnet 24, his " bosom's shop,"
where, on the " table of his heart," the secret hangs
as a " jewel " (Sonnet 27), illumining the surround-
ing darkness of material nature, which, destitute of
the jewel, is compared to " ghastly night."   But the
weakness of man is such that the mere possession of
the secret in " silence " is not always and of itself
enough, and the possessor is sometimes seduced
abroad without his " cloak; " i. e. his hermetic veil
(Sonnet 34), allowing others " to see his pleasure "
(Sonnet 75), which brought the poet into difficulties ;
because the outer world never tolerates a too open
exhibition of truth, though it be in itself the highest
attainment possible to man.

In the 102d Sonnet the poet refers to the open expression of the secret as bringing a taint upon it: " That love is merchandized [says he] whose rich esteeming the owner's tongue doth publish every-where." And he tells us, in the 21st Sonnet, that he has no purpose to " sell,"—to sell what ?—the secret of the Lord—for it is the gift of God, which St. Paul tells us cannot be bought with money. The reader need not be startled at these allusions to the Scripture, for he who brought grace and truth to light, teaches us that the truth *was* before Abraham,—as it now is and shall be for ever.

The 77th Sonnet contains a reference to what the poet calls " this learning," which is no other than hermetic learning ; and this 77th Sonnet, when studied, may show that the secret learning is a true knowledge of one's self, acquired, under the blessing of God, by accurately noticing the interior action of life, as it discloses itself in the soul. We must suppose the poet, in " compiling " the 77th Sonnet, seated with " blank leaves " before him ; and then he addresses himself:

77. Thy glass will show thee how thy beauties wear,
   Thy dial how thy precious minutes waste ;
   These vacant leaves *thy mind's imprint will bear,*
   And of this book

[the book of his own soul]

> this learning may'st thou taste.

> *   *   *   *   *   *   *   *   *   *

> Look, what thy memory cannot contain [retain],
>   Commit to these waste blanks, and thou shalt find
> Those children nurs'd deliver'd from thy brain,
>   To take a new acquaintance of thy mind.
> These offices, so oft as thou wilt look,
> Shall profit thee, and much enrich thy book.

The "book" here spoken of is the man's own soul, the book of life, which is to be profited by the exercises recommended by the poet.

The 48th Sonnet, however, shows that the poet saw how crude and imperfect his first efforts had been in seeking the knowledge of himself, by keeping a note-book; but thus seeing his inadequate efforts, was precisely the evidence of his advance in the direction he was pursuing:

48.   How careful

[says the poet]

> was I when I took my way,
> Each trifle under truest bars to thrust,
> That to my use it might unused stay,
> From hands of falsehood, in sure vards of trust!

That is, the poet was careful, when he first took
his way in life, to keep an accurate *note-book* of,
probably, his outward life, prizing every "trifle" of
it. But when he came to the true knowledge, he
saw that what he had regarded as "jewels," were
but "trifles," to his "greatest grief." He saw that
something, which he had overlooked, was left the
prey to every vulgar thief (or pen) ; and this something he had not locked up in any chest :

> Save where [says he] thou art not, though I feel thou art,
> Within the gentle closure of my breast.

That is, he had been too free with his heart, until
it had become, in some sense, vacant,—the spirit was
not locked up there; and yet, in another sense, the
poet *felt* that it was truly there, "within the
gentle closure of his breast," or what he calls, in the
24th Sonnet, his "bosom's shop,"

> A closet never pierced with crystal eyes. (*Sonnet* 46.)

Sonnets 116 to 120, inclusive, were designed to
illustrate the doctrine of good growing out of evil.
The 120th Sonnet has a perfectly clear meaning in
what may be called its spiritual sense. We must
understand the profound sense of unity conceived by

the poet, through which his own most intimate experiences were seen as having a certain relation, binding them, or the poet himself, to the whole, the One-All. Upon this ground the poet does not hesitate to attribute his suffering to what he calls the *unkindness* of the object addressed; language used, however, only in his transitional state; for the true doctrine of the poet requires him to take all *blames* and *blindness* upon himself (Sonnets 36, 149, etc). The personal suffering of the poet finally awakens in him the conviction, that in his "transgression" he has brought pain upon the higher spirit. The sense of this awakens compunction, coupled with the regret that he had not *sooner* been brought to a certain humble salve, which is no other than a true repentance: for this is the only salve for bosoms wounded by transgression. At length the true insight comes, that his own affliction, the consequence of what he calls a "trespass," had first *liberated* the true spirit (seen through repentance), as if it had been confined within what is often called the natural man (or the natural heart); and then the poet perceives that the spirit, thus liberated, is precisely the spirit which must liberate him, or free him from the dominion of an evil life.

It would be easy to give the popular name to this spirit, by whose sufferings or stripes we are healed; but we leave this for the faithful student, who, if he touches the true sense of these Sonnets, will have touched the deepest depths of life. We will only remark, on this point, that when the Scripture declares, that whom the Lord loveth he chasteneth, we may understand that it is not every suffering that worketh, certainly not directly, the redemption of man, but that only or chiefly which proceeds from the spirit of righteousness, inducing that hunger and thirst spoken of in the sermon on the Mount: "Blessed are they which do hunger and thirst after righteousness, for they shall be filled."

There are some lines in the 61st Sonnet, which may suggest to many readers the true object addressed by the poet.

61. Is it *thy spirit*—

[evidently referring to the "household god," the CONSCIENCE],

> Is it thy spirit that thou send'st from thee
>> So far from home, into my deeds to pry;
> To find out shames and idle hours in me,
>> The scope and tenor of thy jealousy?

It is impossible that these lines could have been addressed to any mere person.

CHAPTER VI.

THERE are yet remaining some points to be further explained. We have expressed the opinion that the opening Sonnets, some sixteen or eighteen, or most of them, may be considered as invocations addressed to the higher spirit of the poet—to what may be called the Muse of Life : " Be thou the tenth muse " (says our poet, in Sonnet 38), " ten times more in worth, than those old nine which rymers invocate." But it must be observed that the poet's prayer is, that he himself may be the medium of expression. This is shown in a multitude of passages, more or less directly, scattered throughout the Sonnets. Thus, in the 21st Sonnet, he says: " O let me, true in love, but truly write." This line is, in some sense, the key-note of his purpose.

A large proportion of the Sonnets are addressed indirectly by the poet to himself: for although he
4

conceived the higher spirit, he conceived it as his
own better part; hence, whilst he posited, so to say,
the dogma of a separation between himself and the
higher spirit, as in Sonnets 36 and 39, yet, in these
same Sonnets, the poet asserts the unity; and therefore it is in harmony with the poet's own view, to
understand him as addressing himself in many of the
Sonnets, even when the form of the language might
imply a separation; he says, Sonnet 39:

> What can mine own praise to mine own self bring ?
> And what is 't but mine own when I praise thee ?

And, again, in the 62d Sonnet, his language is :

> 'T is thee (myself) that for myself I praise.

The Sonnets, indeed, are transparent with this idea;
and if the reader will but once seize the idea of the
unity as it lived in the poet, he will regard the Sonnets as a series of monologues, in which the poet
now addresses the higher spirit, yet as his own better part, and then addresses himself in what we may
call a more human sense, especially in the opening
Sonnets, as if urging himself to do his part—to make
his own proper effort—at " compiling " verses, to the
honor of love.

It should be kept in mind that it is a poet that

writes, and in the earlier Sonnets we may see him in
the act of asking that inspiration of the spirit which
is necessary to secure a perpetuity for his verses.
The 1st Sonnet is addressed to what the poet calls
Beauty's Rose.   This is a figurative expression for
man, seen in his essential nature, and not simply in
his material and phenomenal structure.   Man is the
Rose of Nature, seen in her beauty.   He is the
crowning beauty of nature, and is hence figuratively
called Beauty's Rose.   He is the *subject* of the 19th
Sonnet, where we see that "devouring Time" is
forbid, as a most heinous crime, from carving the
fair brow of the Rose with her hours, and commanded to draw no lines there with his antique pen;
adding,

> Him in thy course untainted do allow,
>   For beauty's pattern to succeeding men."

This is what the poet saw in the tales of chivalry,
as referred to in the 106th Sonnet, and what he was
prospectively anxious about in the 32d Sonnet.
This was what he saw as "extant" in his own day, in
the 83d Sonnet; and as an "example," or *exemplar*,
in the 84th Sonnet, precisely in the sense of the 19th
Sonnet, as beauty's pattern, to wit, man, as seen in

his pure being; for what is there in nature more wonderful than man; or, in his perfected nature, more beautiful !

The 2d Sonnet is addressed to the poet himself, though its structure seems to convey the idea that the poet is addressing another; but *he is that other*, though in a mystical sense. The simple meaning is this: the poet is giving himself a sort of warning, in the form of a rebuke for not putting his ideal into poetic form. The "fair child" referred to is the child or *heir* of genius, as conceived in some poetic production. The poet is striving to bring himself to the point of expressing in adequate form his *ideal* of beauty, as the spirit of life; urging that, when forty winters shall have passed over him, it would be " an all-eating shame " not to have it in his power to point to some work, in a poetic field, as the evidence of his not having neglected his great endowment of genius, of whose presence he was conscious.

In the 3d Sonnet the word *mother* is twice used, but in different senses. In the fourth line it means simply a *subject* (in nature) for poetic invention to work upon, in a sense similar to that of an expression in the 16th Sonnet, where the poet speaks of *maiden gardens ;* this expression signifying maiden, or virgin, that is, *unwrought*-upon subjects, suitable for the genius of a poet to exercise itself upon.

In the 9th line, Sonnet 3, the poet is himself the "glass"—the glass of nature, nature being the *mother*. The simple idea here is, that the poet felt himself to have been a true child of nature; and in this idea he realized the *beauty*, which he felt ought not to be lost to the world, but should be expressed in some work of art, called an "image" of the beauty he contemplated in man.

The 4th Sonnet has a similar meaning, and furnishes a fine illustration of the parable of the talents in the gospel; teaching that talents, not money, but mental powers, unexercised, must be lost; they are said to be taken from the sluggard and given to the industrious; and this is not by an arbitrary will, but by a law of nature.

There is a passage in Measure for Measure which not only furnishes a fine comment upon the 4th Sonnet, but will go far toward demonstrating that the opening Sonnets had no view to a fleshly progeny, and will explain also much of the language employed in them, especially in the 1st Sonnet :

> But thou, contracted to thine own bright eyes,
>   Feed'st thy light's flame with self-substantial fuel,
> Making a famine where abundance lies,
>   Thyself thy foe, to thy sweet self too cruel.
>
>   *   *   *   *   *   *
>
> Pity the world, or else this glutton be,
> To eat the world's due, by the grave and thee.

In the 1st Scene of Act 1st (Measure for Measure), the Duke clothes Angelo with his full power to act in his stead during his proposed absence from Vienna, and, in tendering his commission, he addresses Angelo as follows:

>   *   * Thyself and thy belongings
> Are not thine own so proper, as to waste
> Thyself upon thy virtues, them on thee.
> Heaven doth with us, as we with torches do,
> Not light them for ourselves ; for if our virtues
> Did not go forth of us, 't were all alike
> As if we had them not. Spirits are not finely touch'd,
> But to fine issues ; nor *nature never lends*
> The smallest scruple of her excellence,
> But, like a thrifty goddess, she determines
> Herself the glory of a creditor,
> Both thanks and use.

In the 4th Sonnet we read:

4. Unthrifty loveliness, why dost thou spend
   Upon thyself thy beauty's legacy?
Nature's bequest gives nothing, but *doth lend*,
   And being frank, she lends to those are free, etc.

To see the application of the passage from Measure for Measure, we have only to suppose that Beauty's Rose, or a sense of the Beautiful, is the endowment of the poet, nature's " loan," which must be put to use, or it must be lost.

The 5th Sonnet has a similar meaning : the poet is simply warning himself that, unless he *expresses* himself, meaning as a poet, his ideal of beauty will be lost to the world, but, if he will write (the idea is), he shall live in his writings after what, in the 74th Sonnet, he calls his " show," that is, his *body*, shall perish. This will appear very plainly the true meaning from the 74th Sonnet.

The 6th Sonnet has the same purpose : the 7th has also a similar purpose, the " son " being some work of art.

In like manner the 8th, 9th, 10th, 11th, 12th, and 13th are so many persuasions addressed by the poet himself to himself, to beget a copy of himself in a poetic sense ; precisely as expressed in the 74th Sonnet, as if accomplished.

The root-idea is perfectly simple, but the application is exceedingly complicated.

The poet, in speaking, assumes the entire unity which he conceives: he sometimes addresses that unity, and then again, what may be called the elements of the composite nature of man. Thus, in the 146th Sonnet, the poet addresses his own soul (surely himself), and calls it the centre of *his* sinful earth, which is also himself, in another sense.

The 18th Sonnet contains a key-line (the 12th), similar to that of the 9th in Sonnet 21. The poet here addresses the higher spirit; which is to be placed beyond the power of death, by being made to " grow " to time in " eternal lines."

The 78th Sonnet has already been referred to, in which the poet attributes whatever he " compiles " (or writes), to the *influence* of the object addressed, and speaks of it as having been *born* of that object.

Let the reader compare the 12th and 65th Sonnets, and he will see that the " breed " spoken of in the 12th Sonnet, is not a mortal son; but it is Beauty expressed by means of " black ink " in " immortal verse: " or, as expressed in the 63d Sonnet,

His beauty shall in these black lines be seen, .
And these shall live, and he in them still green.

It is comparatively a paltry view to suppose, in these Sonnets, that the poet was addressing a contemporary person, either male or female. His *ideal*, that which the poet contemplated as Beauty, or the Beautiful, was the object of his prayerful *watchings*, as expressed in the 27th and 61st Sonnets:

27. Weary with toil, I haste me to my bed,
　　The dear repose for limbs with travail tir'd;
　　But then begins a journey in my head,
　　To work my mind, when body's work 's expired:
　　For then my thoughts (from far where I abide)
　　Intend a zealous pilgrimage to thee,
　　And keep my drooping eyelids open wide,
　　Looking on darkness, which the blind do see;
　　Save that my soul's imaginary sight
　　Presents thy shadow to my sightless view,
　　Which, *like a jewel hung in ghastly night,*
　　Makes black night beauteous, and her old face new.
　　　Lo, thus, by day my limbs, by night my mind,
　　　For thee, and for myself, no quiet find.

61. Is it thy will, thy image should keep open
　　My heavy eyelids to the weary night?
　　　4*

Dost thou desire my slumbers should be broken,
While shadows, like to thee, do mock my sight?
Is it thy spirit that thou send'st from thee
So far from home, into my deeds to pry?
To find out shames and idle hours in me,
The scope and tenour of thy jealousy?
O no! thy love, though much, is not so great;
It is my love that keeps mine eye awake;
Mine own true love that doth my rest defeat,
To play the watchman ever for thy sake:
  For thee watch I, whilst thou dost wake elsewhere,
  From me far off, with others all too near.

In order to realize something of the nature of
these two Sonnets, the reader has only to consider
an instance of his own desire for the accomplish-
ment of some darling purpose of a worldly character; and then let him imagine a change of
object, and allow that while some men devote
themselves, body and soul, to effect what may
be called worldly objects, having reference to
time, others, though few in number, like those
who enter the strait way, may equally devote
themselves to the attainment of a certain object
which, for convenience, may be called spiritual
and eternal. This spiritual aspiration is what
the poet, in the 61st Sonnet, calls his "own love,"

which compels him to "play the watchman,"—
truly not unlike the fulfilment of the repeated
injunctions of Scripture—to watch and pray always; we do not say, in precisely the sense of the
Scripture command, yet not unlike it.

If after the interpretations we have given the
opinion should still be persevered in; that the Sonnets under examination were addressed to some
merely human person contemporary with the poet,
we should be disposed to wonder how such a
student is to be convinced that God is a Spirit, the
Spirit of all-embracing life which knows no death;
in the "heart" of which our poet sought to be
obsequious (Sonnet 125), wherein he saw what was
of more value in his eyes than "all this wide universe besides" (Sonnet 109), as shown in the following Sonnets:

29. When in disgrace with fortune and men's eyes,
    I all alone beweep my outcast state,
    And trouble deaf heaven with my bootless cries,
    And look upon myself and curse my fate,
    Wishing me like to one more rich in hope,
    Featur'd like him, like him with friends possess'd,
    Desiring this man's art, and that man's scope,
    With what I most enjoy contented least;

Yet in these thoughts myself almost despising,
Haply I think on thee,—and then my state
(Like to the lark at break of day arising
From sullen earth) sings hymns at heaven's gate ;
   For thy sweet love remember'd, such wealth brings,
   That then I scorn to change my state with kings.

30. When to the sessions of sweet silent thought
I summon up remembrance of things past,
I sigh the lack of many a thing I sought,
And with old woes new wail my dear times' waste :
Then can I drown an eye, unus'd to flow,
For precious friends hid in death's dateless night,
And weep afresh love's long-since cancell'd woe,
And moan the expense of many a vanish'd sight.
Then can I grieve at grievances foregone,
And heavily from woe to woe tell o'er
The sad account of fore-bemoaned moan,
Which I new pay as if not paid before.
   But if the while I think on thee, dear friend,
   All losses are restored, and sorrows end.

31. Thy bosom is endeared with all hearts,
Which I by lacking have supposed dead ;
And there reigns love and all love's loving parts,
And all those friends which I thought buried.
How many a holy and obsequious tear
Hath dear religious love stolen from mine eye,

As interest of the dead. which now appear
But things remov'd, that hidden in thee lie !
Thou art the grave where buried love doth live,
Hung with the trophies of my lovers gone,
Who all their parts of me to thee did give;
That due of many now is thine alone :
   Their images I lov'd I view in thee,
   And thou (all they) hast all the all of me.

Can we not now, at least theoretically—and we do not feel bound to defend any man's doctrines of life—can we not now understand enough of the doctrines of the poet, to perceive, with deeply interesting appreciation, the general purpose of the Sonnets, and that, in some sort, they tell us of the poet's interior life in its joys and triumphs, and no less in its sorrows and trials? We are fully persuaded that we have nothing in profane literature, of the same extent, more deserving profound study than the Sonnets we have had under examination.

It is not denied but that many of them may easily be understood as applicable to ordinary life, even where a higher purpose was designed; but we are well assured that the general explanation applicable to most of them requires the supposition of a mystical object, called in the 1st Sonnet Beauty's

Rose, which is not found in any one distinct visible object in the world; for which reason Moses forbid the children of Israel from making any image of it, in the likeness of anything that is in the heavens above, or in the earth beneath, or in the waters under the earth.

CHAPTER VII.

WE have already drawn a few illustrations of the Sonnets from the dramas of the poet, but there is one, and a very important one, in Midsummer-Night's Dream, which must on no account be omitted.

The author of these Remarks had the pleasure of being well acquainted with the late talented and most unfortunate Miss Bacon, prior to the publication of her volume on the works of Shakespeare, and while her peculiar views were germinating in her mind. He had much conversation at the time with that accomplished lady, and heard with more curiosity, as he confesses, than interest, some of her opinions. He remembers particularly that Midsummer-Night's Dream was one of the dramas selected by Miss Bacon for illustrating her theory, not indeed as to the authorship of the dramas, but as to their interior signification. He has, however, no distinct recollection of her interpretation of the plays, nor has he read her volume on the subject subsequently published. The writer remembers that she attributed the plays to Lord Bacon, and was of opinion that the dramas, or some of them, were designed to express certain philosophic opinions in an esoteric form, that form being selected because the age would not tolerate an open publication of them. In this connection it is proper to refer to the 66th Sonnet, which contains an enumeration of many evils of the time, among which one was that Art was tongue-tied by authority ; which may be thought some confirmation of Miss Bacon's views.

The author has no distinct recollection as to what the doctrines were, thus hidden, according to Miss Bacon, from common observation. He makes this statement in order to add, that while he has not consciously adopted any of Miss Bacon's opinions, he would be more than content to find himself in her company on the single point he proposes to confirm from the Interlude in the 5th Act of Midsummer-Night's Dream. The author had no thought of the peculiar opinions of Miss Bacon when he fell upon the idea here expressed of the Sonnets. He is not aware that Miss Bacon included the Sonnets within the range of her inquiries; nor does he know whether the Sonnets are touched upon in her book, or what opinion she entertained of them.

For the writer's present purpose it is necessary to re-state a portion of his view of the Sonnets, as presented in the preceding chapters.

He is of opinion that the Sonnets express, in an abstract though mystical form, the speculative opinions of the author of the dramas; not, indeed, as final results, but up to the period in life, whenever that was, when the poet ceased to write Sonnets. The Sonnets themselves do not exhibit what may be called ultimate views of life, except as such views are seen in a mystery. It is very plain that no man, living in the flesh, can speak of death from experience. Hence the Sonnets do not carry forward the poet's view to final opinions. They carry the attentive reader to a point where the poet, finding himself painfully entangled in the mysteries of life, sought relief in what he calls the "seething bath" (Sonnet 153), and finding no relief, as he tells us, he became convinced of the necessity, as if laid upon himself individually, of seeking "help where Cupid

got new fire, [his] mistress' eyes." What help the
poet found from that quarter, or whether he found
any, he does not inform us; upon which fact it is
proper to observe that the Sonnets do not carry with
them authoritative instruction, though they are emi-
nently suggestive and full of real instruction to a
thoughtful reader.

Now, the doctrine of the Sonnets, as we have
attempted to show, is substantially this: that the
spirit of man is one with the spirit of nature; as
may be seen more particularly by a careful study of
the 39th and 74th Sonnets, though this doctrine is
quite manifest in many of the Sonnets.

A sense of this unity was the secret joy of the
poet, taking the name of love. This was, to the
poet, better than high birth, richer than wealth,
prouder than garments' cost, of more delight than
hawks or horses; and having that, he felt that he
could boast of all men's pride, etc. (Sonnet 91).
This sense of unity prompted the 25th Sonnet:

> 25. Let those who are in favor with their stars,
>   Of public honor and proud titles boast,
>   Whilst I, whom fortune of such triumph bars,
>   Unlook'd for, joy in *that* I honor most.

Great princes' favorites their fair leaves spread,
But as the marigold at the sun's eye ;
And in themselves their pride lies buried,
For at a frown they in their glory die.
The painful warrior famoused for fight,
After a thousand victories once foiled,
Is from the book of honor razed quite,
And all the rest forgot for which he toiled :
    Then happy I, that love and am beloved,
    Where *I may not remove nor be removed.*

The sense of this unity threw a beauty over all
external nature, giving it the appearance of being but
" the seemly raiment of the poet's heart " (Sonnet
22).   It annihilated death, as we see in the 30th and
31st Sonnets.   It gave the poet strength to realize
his independence, even to the point of declaring, in
the language of Scripture, " I am that I am " (Sonnet 121) ; and enabled him to make the great affirma-
tion in contempt of the boast of time—" I will be
true, despite thy scythe and thee."

But whilst this sense of unity runs through the
Sonnets as one of their principal secrets, the poet felt
a disturbing presence, the presence of something
which obscured his vision ; a sense of something as
if interposed between himself or his own spirit, and
the universal spirit, or that which, adopting the

happy phrase of Emerson, we may call the Over-
Soul. This interposed obstacle, standing in the way
of the poet, is called in the 44th Sonnet the "dull
substance of the flesh," and is no other than material
nature, which stands, as it were, between the two
spirits like a *wall* of separation. Hence it is called
in the 36th Sonnet a "separable" (or separating)
spite.

The poet felt that he loved the spirit of nature,
which flitted before his mind's eye as the spirit of
Beauty; and he believed in the unity of his own
with that spirit; while yet he realized something
that disturbed his vision, which, as he tells us, in the
20th Sonnet, was "nothing to his purpose," calling
it "an addition," which threw a veil over the otherwise feminine beauty of the spirit.

This mysterious, and, to the poet's "purpose,"
this unnecessary "addition," appears everywhere in
the Sonnets as a sort of foil to the spirit, but without
adding beauty to it. It is everywhere an obstacle
in the estimate of the poet. It is the "painted beauty" of the 21st Sonnet. Whatever beauty it has, it
receives from the poet's heart, seeming like its raiment, Sonnet 22. The eye paints its beauty upon
the table of the heart, Sonnet 24, yet the eye is said

to want a certain " cunning "— it " knows not the
heart." This " dull substance" is what does not
permit the " soul's thought " to stand "all naked "
(Sonnet 26) ; and thus prevents the poet from dedi-
cating his verse to the praise of love. It makes the
" ghastly night " of the 27th Sonnet, and the
" clouds," blotting heaven, of the 28th Sonnet ; and
the " basest clouds " of the 33d Sonnet, said to pass
over the " celestial face" of the spirit. This was what
compelled the poet to acknowledge that he and his
love must be twain ; while yet he felt that their undivided (or indivisible) loves were one, Sonnet 36.
It was this fleshy substance that made the conflict
between the eye and heart, as in the 46th Sonnet,
and drew from the poet's heart the decision that to
the eye belonged the *outward* part, while the heart's
right claimed the *inward* love of heart. The same
" dull substance " is the " beast " of the 50th Sonnet,
which drew the poet away from his love, the spirit.
This was what made the " winter " of the 56th Sonnet, in whose presence the poet tried to see a virtue,
in that it made the summer's (or spirit's) welcome
thrice more wished, more rare. It is the poet himself who felt, in the dull substance of the flesh, what
he calls, in the 58th Sonnet, the "imprisoned ab-

sence " of liberty; but which, in a sublime spirit of resignation, he implores he may suffer in " patience," without accusing the higher spirit of injury.

The " dull substance," the source of " impiety," is the " infection " with which the spirit was seen to live, moving the profoundest sigh of the poet, as in Sonnet 67; and yet a conscious sense of the presence of the spirit turned all defects to beauties, as may be seen in several of the Sonnets; for it is only in a true sense of the spirit that the obliquities of life find their true solution.

The "dull substance " is the canopy of the spirit of the 125th Sonnet, which the poet wished to throw aside, that he might live in that unity of the spirit, which " is not mixed with *seconds*," and, in its own simple truth, " knows no art; " or, as expressed in the 78th Sonnet, it is the poet's " only art "—evidently that of truth and beauty, or " truth in beauty dy'd." Sonnets 54, 101.

The object addressed in the Sonnets is essentially conceived as a unity, designated in the 1st Sonnet, by a figurative expression, as Beauty's Rose; but it is unavoidably realized as double, and is thence called, in the 20th Sonnet, the master-mistress of the poet's passion, or love; the master side, so to say, being the spirit, in which the unity is seen, while the " addition," or dull substance of the flesh, is regarded as the *separating* something which the poet struggles to lose sight of in the spirit. It appears, at times, clothed with the beauty of the spirit, and then, at another time, it wears a gloomy aspect—" as dark as night, as black as hell."

Here are three, the spirit in man, the dull substance of the flesh, and the over-soul, " and these three are conceived as one," but with a disturbing sense of the body interposed, as it were, between the two spirits, where it stands like a *wall* of separation, the wall being now conceived of as the man, and then as the vestment of the universe itself—which, as we read, is to be rolled up like a scroll, etc., when God shall be all in all.

This consummation does not appear in the Sonnets themselves, though, as a doctrine, it is everywhere implied by the poet's deep sense of the unity. It is mystically shown, however, in the ancient fable of Pyramus and Thisbe, as the reader is expected to see by the manner in which the poet uses that fable in the Interlude introduced in the closing Act of Midsummer-Night's Dream.

It may not be amiss to remind the reader of the

dramas that it was usual with our poet to express the most profound truths through dramatic characters, and yet partially screen them from common inspection by the circumstances, or the sort of character made the vehicle of them—such as Jaques and others. The reader need not be surprised therefore to find the *dramatis personæ* of the " merry and tragical" Interlude to be boorish and idiotic, while it is worth remarking that even the *wall*, as also the other parts, are all represented by men, unconscious of their calling.

We now turn to the drama, and remark, that it was designed by the poet that a secret meaning should be inferred by the reader. This appears from several very decisive passages, besides the general inference to be drawn from the fact, that the Interlude in the 5th Act of the drama, more than all the rest of the play, if taken literally, is what Hippolyta says of it—the silliest stuff that was ever seen. No reasonable man can imagine that the author of so many beauties as are seen in this drama, could have introduced the absurd nonsense of the Interlude without having in his mind a secret purpose, which is to be divined by the aid of the reader's imagination—

according to the answer of Theseus to the remark of
Hippolyta, just recited. But the imagination must
here be understood as a poetic creative gift or endowment, and not limited to mere "fancy's images;" for
Hippolyta herself, though here speaking of the play,
gives us a clue to something deeper than what
appears on the surface. She, in allusion to all the
marvels the bridal party had just heard, observes,

> But all the story of the *night* told over,
> And all their minds transfigured so together,
> *More witnesseth than fancy's images,*
> *And grows to something of great constancy.*

This is plainly a hint that these "fables and
fairy toys," as Theseus calls them, may be the
vehicle of some *constant* truth or principle.
     Again:

> Gentles, perchance you wonder at this show;
> But wonder on, till truth make all things plain.

That is, when the truth, signified in the "show,"
becomes manifest, all wonder will cease, for the object of its introduction will be understood.
     When Hippolyta pronounces the show "silly
stuff," which, of course, it is, unless there be a secret
     5

purpose, Theseus answers: "The best in this kind
are but shadows; and the worst are no worse, if
imagination amend them;" that is, as we have said,
the "show" calls for the exercise of the poetic or
creative imagination to bring the kernel out of the
husk or shell in which it is presented by the show.
The poet himself has told us, in the drama itself, the action of the so-called gift, when he describes the poet's
eye, in a fine frenzy rolling, as glancing from heaven
to earth, and from earth to heaven, and as imagination bodies forth the forms of things unknown, the
poet's pen turns them to shapes, and "gives to airy
nothing a local habitation and a name." But in these
airy nothings of the poet are to be found some of
the truest revelations of life.

We consider now, that we have no need to dwell
upon the points in detail suggested by the closing
Act of the drama, which contains the doctrine we
have set out as mystically contained in the Sonnets.
The curious reader, who desires to exercise his own
thought, while following that of the poet, expressed
through the imprisoning forms of language, will see,
with the indications we have given, the purpose of
the "mirthful tragedy" of Pyramus and Thisbe.
He will see the signification of the two characters or

principles, figured in Pyramus and Thisbe, with the
wall, "the vile wall which did these lovers sunder."
Through this *wall* (the dull substance of the flesh),
the lovers may indeed communicate, but only by a
" whisper, very secretly; " because the intercourse of
spirit with spirit is a secret act of the soul in a sense
of its unity with the spirit.   The student will readily
catch the meaning of the "moon-shine," or *nature*-
light, in this representation, the moon being always
taken as nature in all mystic writings.   He will see
the symbolism of the " dog "—the *watch*-dog, of
course,—representing the moral guard in a nature-
life; as also the bush of *thorns*, ever ready to illustrate the doctrine that the way of the transgressor
is hard.   The student will notice the hint that the
lovers meet by moonlight and at a tomb—a symbolic indication of the greatest mystery in life (to be
found in death); and he will understand the office of
the lion, which tears, not Thisbe herself, but only her
" mantle," or what the poet calls the " extern " of life;
and finally will observe that the two principles both
disappear; for the unity cannot become mystically
visible, until the two principles are mystically lost
sight of.

It should not escape notice that the two principles are co-equal; that "a mote will turn the balance, which Pyramus, which Thisbe, is the better"—simply figured as man and woman.

The student of Midsummer-Night's Dream may observe two very marked features in the play; one, in the 1st Scene of the 2d Act, where the "juice," which induces so many absurdities, cross-purposes, and monstrosities, is described as the juice of (a certain flower called love-in-) *idleness:* the other, in the 1st Scene of the 4th Act, where we see that all of the irregularities resulting from idleness are cured by the simple anointment of the eyes by what is called "Dian's bud"—which has such "force and blessed power" as to bring all of the faculties back to nature and truth,—of which Dian is one of the accepted figures in all mystic writings.

The readers of this play, who look upon these indications as purely arbitrary and without distinct meaning, may, indeed, perceive some of the scattered beauties of this *fairy* drama, but must certainly miss its true import.

SHAKESPEARE'S SONNETS.

TO

THE ONLY BEGETTER OF THESE ENSUING SONNETS,

Mr. W. H.,

ALL HAPPINESS

AND

THAT ETERNITY PROMISED BY OUR EVER-LIVING POET,

WISHETH

THE WELL-WISHING ADVENTURER

IN SETTING FORTH,

T. T.*

* T. T.—That is, Thomas Thorpe, the original publisher.

In reading the Sonnets, the Author of the Remarks found it convenient to make notes of reference from Sonnet to Sonnet where he saw either parallel or contrasted passages, tending to illustrate their general sense; and these references are here added, as some gratification, he hopes, to the curious and studious.

[The Sonnets are taken from the edition of Shakespeare's Works edited by Mrs. Mary Cowden Clarke.]

SHAKESPEARE'S SONNETS.

I.

From fairest creatures we desire increase,
That thereby beauty's rose might never die,
But as the riper should by time decease,
His tender heir might bear his memory:
But thou, contracted to thine own bright eyes,
Feed'st thy light's flame with self-substantial fuel,
Making a famine where abundance lies,
Thyself thy foe, to thy sweet self too cruel.
Thou that art now the world's fresh ornament,
And only herald to the gaudy spring,
Within thine own bud buriest thy content,
And, tender churl, mak'st waste in niggarding.

    Pity the world, or else this glutton be,
    To eat the world's due, by the grave and thee.

Vide Remarks, pp. 18, 20 : also Sonnet 78.

5*

II.

When forty winters shall besiege thy brow,
And dig deep trenches in thy beauty's field,
Thy youth's proud livery, so gaz'd on now,
Will be a tatter'd weed, of small worth held:
Then being ask'd where all thy beauty lies,
Where all the treasure of thy lusty days,—
To say, within thine own deep sunken eyes,
Were an all-eating shame and thriftless praise.
How much more praise deserv'd thy beauty's use,
If thou couldst answer—"This fair child of mine
Shall sum my count, and make my old excuse,—"
Proving his beauty by succession thine!

    This were to be new-made when thou art old,
    And see thy blood warm when thou feel'st it cold.

Vide REMARKS, p. 76 : also Sonnets 63, 64, 78, 81.

III.

Look in thy glass, and tell the face thou viewest,
Now is the time that face should form another;
Whose fresh repair if now thou not renewest,
Thou dost beguile the world, unbless some mother.
For where is she so fair whose unear'd womb
Disdains the tillage of thy husbandry?
Or who is he so fond will be the tomb
Of his self-love, to stop posterity?
Thou art thy mother's glass, and she in thee
Calls back the lovely April of her prime:
So thou through windows of thine age shalt see,
Despite of wrinkles, this thy golden time.

But if thou live, remember'd not to be,
Die single, and thine image dies with thee.

Vide REMARKS, pp. 16, 76, 77 : also Sonnets 77, 78.

IV.

Unthrifty loveliness, why dost thou spend
Upon thyself thy beauty's legacy?
Nature's bequest gives nothing, but doth lend;
And, being frank, she lends to those are free.
Then, beauteous niggard, why dost thou abuse
The bounteous largess given thee to give?
Profitless usurer, why dost thou use
So great a sum of sums, yet canst not live?
For having traffic with thyself alone,
Thou of thyself thy sweet self dost deceive.
Then how, when nature calls thee to be gone,
What acceptable audit canst thou leave?

  Thy unus'd beauty must be tomb'd with thee,
  Which, used, lives th' executor to be.

Vide REMARKS, pp. 77-79: also Sonnet 36.

V.

Those hours, that with gentle work did frame
The lovely gaze where every eye doth dwell,
Will play the tyrants to the very same,
And that unfair which fairly doth excel;
For never-resting time leads summer on
To hideous winter, and confounds him there;
Sap check'd with frost, and lusty leaves quite gone,
Beauty o'ersnow'd, and bareness everywhere:
Then, were not summer's distillation left,
A liquid prisoner pent in walls of glass,
Beauty's effect with beauty were bereft,
Nor it, nor no remembrance what it was:

But flowers distill'd, though they with winter meet,
Leese but their show; their substance still lives sweet.

Vide REMARKS, p. 79 : also Sonnets 54, 64, 74.

VI.

Then let not winter's ragged hand deface
In thee thy summer, ere thou be distill'd:
Make sweet some phial; treasure thou some place
With beauty's treasure, ere it be self-kill'd.
That use is not forbidden usury,
Which happies those that pay the willing loan;
That 's for thyself to breed another thee,
Or ten times happier, be it ten for one;
Ten times thyself were happier than thou art,
If ten of thine ten times refigur'd thee:
Then what could death do, if thou shouldst depart,
Leaving thee living in posterity?

 Be not self-will'd, for thou art much too fair
 To be Death's conquest, and make worms thine heir,

Vide Sonnets 5, 54, 74, 78.

VII.

Lo, in the orient when the gracious light
Lifts up his burning head, each under eye
Doth homage to his new-appearing sight,
Serving with looks his sacred majesty; .
And having climb'd the steep-up heavenly hill,
Resembling strong youth in his middle age,
Yet mortal looks adore his beauty still,
Attending on his golden pilgrimage;
But when from high-most pitch, with weary car,
Like feeble age, he reeleth from the day,
The eyes, 'fore duteous, now converted are
From his low tract, and look another way:
   So thou, thyself outgoing in thy noon,
    Unlook'd on diest, unless thou get a son.

Vide Sonnets 55, 78, 107.

VIII.

Music to hear, why hear'st thou music sadly?
Sweets with sweets war not, joy delights in joy.
Why lov'st thou that which thou receiv'st not gladly,
Or else receiv'st with pleasure thine annoy?
If the true concord of well-tuned sounds,
By unions married, do offend thine ear,
They do but sweetly chide thee, who confounds
In singleness the parts that thou shouldst bear.
Mark how one string, sweet husband to another,
Strikes each in each by mutual ordering;
Resembling sire and child and happy mother,
Who, all in one, one pleasing note do sing:

    Whose speechless song, being many, seeming one,
    Sings this to thee, "thou single wilt prove none."

Vide Sonnet 59.

IX.

Is it for fear to wet a widow's eye
That thou consum'st thyself in single life?
Ah! if thou issueless shalt hap to die,
The world will wail thee, like a makeless wife;
The world will be thy widow, and still weep
That thou no form of thee hast left behind,
When every private widow well may keep,
By children's eyes, her husband's shape in mind.
Look, what an unthrift in the world doth spend,
Shifts but his place, for still the world enjoys it;
But beauty's waste hath in the world an end,
And kept unus'd, the user so destroys it.

    No love toward others in that bosom sits,
      That on himself such murderous shame commits.

Vide Sonnets 60, 74, 78.

X.

For shame ! deny that thou bear'st love to any,
Who for thyself art so unprovident.
Grant, if thou wilt, thou art belov'd of many,
But that thou none lov'st is most evident;
For thou art so possess'd with murderous hate,
That 'gainst thyself thou stick'st not to conspire,
Seeking that beauteous roof to ruinate,
Which to repair should be thy chief desire.
O, change thy thought, that I may change my mind!
Shall hate be fairer lodg'd than gentle love?
Be, as thy presence is, gracious and kind,
Or to thyself, at least, kind-hearted prove:
     Make thee another self, for love of me,
      That beauty still may live in thine or thee.

Vide Sonnets 74, 78.

XI.

As fast as thou shalt wane, so fast thou growest
In one of thine, from that which thou departest;
And that fresh blood which youngly thou bestowest,
Thou mayst call thine, when thou from youth convertest.
Herein lives wisdom, beauty, and increase;
Without this, folly, age, and cold decay:
If all were minded so, the times should cease,
And threescore years would make the world away.
Let those whom Nature hath not made for store,
Harsh, featureless, and rude, barrenly perish
Look, whom she best endow'd, she gave the more;
Which bounteous gift thou shouldst in bounty cherish:
 She carved thee for her seal, and meant thereby
 Thou shouldst print more, not let that copy die.

Vide Sonnets 54, 126.

XII.

When I do count the clock that tells the time,
And see the brave day sunk in hideous night;
When I behold the violet past prime,
And sable curls all silver'd o'er with white;
When lofty trees I see barren of leaves,
Which erst from heat did canopy the herd,
And summer's green, all girded up in sheaves,
Borne on the bier with white and bristly beard;
Then of thy beauty do I question make,
That thou among the wastes of time must go,
Since sweets and beauties do themselves forsake,
And die as fast as they see others grow;

    And nothing 'gainst Time's scythe can make defence
    Save breed, to brave him when he takes thee hence.

Vide REMARKS, p. 79 : also Sonnets 65, 78.

XIII.

O, that you were yourself ! but, love, you are
No longer yours than you yourself here live :
Against this coming end you should prepare,
And your sweet semblance to some other give.
So should that beauty which you hold in lease
Find no determination ; then you were
Yourself again, after yourself's decease,
When your sweet issue your sweet form should bear.
Who lets so fair a house fall to decay,
Which husbandry in honour might uphold
Against the stormy gusts of winter's day, .
And barren rage of death's eternal cold!
    O, none but unthrifts :—dear my love, you know
    You had a father ; let your son say so.

Vide Sonnets 63, 74, 78, 81.

* XIV.

Not from the stars do I my judgment pluck;
And yet methinks I have astronomy,
But not to tell of good or evil luck,
Of plagues, of dearths, or season's quality;
Nor can I fortune to brief minutes tell,
Pointing to each his thunder, rain, and wind,
Or say with princes if it shall go well,
By oft predict that I in heaven find:
But from thine eyes my knowledge I derive,
And, constant stars, in them I read such art,
As truth and beauty shall together thrive,
If from thyself to store thou wouldst convert;
    Or else of thee this I prognosticate,—
    Thy end is truth's and beauty's doom and date.

Vide Sonnets 49, 54.

XV.

When I consider every thing that grows
Holds in perfection but a little moment,
That this huge stage presenteth naught but shows,
Whereon the stars in secret influence comment;
When I perceive that men as plants increase,
Cheered and check'd even by the selfsame sky,
Vaunt in their youthful sap, at height decrease,
And wear their brave state out of memory;
Then the conceit of this inconstant stay
Sets you most rich in youth before my sight,
Where wasteful time debateth with decay,
To change your day of youth to sullied night;
 And, all in war with Time, for love of you,
 As he takes from you, I engraft you new.

Vide Sonnets 37, 82, 100, 101.

XVI.

But wherefore do not you a mightier way
Make war upon this bloody tyrant, Time?
And fortify yourself in your decay
With means more blessed than my barren rhyme?
Now stand you on the top of happy hours;
And many maiden gardens, yet unset,
With virtuous wish would bear your living flowers,
Much liker than your painted counterfeit:
So should the lines of life that life repair,
Which this, Time's pencil, or my pupil pen,
Neither in inward worth, nor outward fair,
Can make you live yourself in eyes of men.

    To give away yourself keeps yourself still;
    And you must live, drawn by your own sweet skill.

Vide REMARKS, pp. 16, 23, 76 · also Sonnets 26, 38, 78, 79, 84, 101, 125, 126, 150.

XVII.

Who will believe my verse in time to come,
If it were fill'd with your most high deserts?
Though yet, Heaven knows, it is but as a tomb
Which hides your life, and shows not half your parts.
If I could write the beauty of your eyes,
And in fresh numbers number all your graces,
The age to come would say, "this poet lies,
Such heavenly touches ne'er touch'd earthly faces."
So should my papers, yellow'd with their age,
Be scorn'd, like old men of less truth than tongue;
And your true rights be term'd a poet's rage,
And stretched metre of an antique song:
　　But were some child of yours alive that time,
　　You should live twice,—in it, and in my rhyme.

Vide Sonnets 78, 83, 103.

XVIII.

Shall I compare thee to a summer's day?
Thou art more lovely and more temperate:
Rough winds do shake the darling buds of May,
And summer's lease hath all too short a date:
Sometime too hot the eye of heaven shines,
And often is his gold complexion dimm'd;
And every fair from fair sometime declines,
By chance, or nature's changing course, untrimm'd;
But thy eternal summer shall not fade,
Nor lose possession of that fair thou owest;
Nor shall Death brag thou wander'st in his shade,
When in eternal lines to time thou growest:

    So long as men can breathe, or eyes can see,
    So long lives this, and this gives life to thee.

Vide REMARKS, p. 80: also Sonnets 53, 60, 123.

XIX.

Devouring Time, blunt thou the lion's paws,
And make the earth devour her own sweet brood;
Pluck the keen teeth from the fierce tiger's jaws,
And burn the long-liv'd phœnix in her blood;
Make glad and sorry seasons as thou fleets,
And do whate'er thou wilt, swift-footed Time,
To the wide world, and all her fading sweets;
But I forbid thee one most heinous crime:
O, carve not with thy hours my love's fair brow,
Nor draw no lines there with thine antique pen;
Him in thy course untainted do allow,
For beauty's pattern to succeeding men.

    Yet, do thy worst, old Time; despite thy wrong,
    My love shall in my verse ever live young.

Vide REMARKS, p. 75 : also Sonnet 83.

XX.

A woman's face, with nature's own hand painted,
Hast thou, the master-mistress of my passion;
A woman's gentle heart, but not acquainted
With shifting change, as is false women's fashion;
An eye more bright than theirs, less false in rolling,
Gilding the object whereupon it gazeth;
A man in hue, all hues in his controlling,
Which steals men's eyes, and women's souls amazeth.
And for a woman wert thou first created;
Till Nature, as she wrought thee, fell a-doting,
And by addition me of thee defeated,
By adding one thing to my purpose nothing.

    But since she prick'd thee out for women's pleasure,
    Mine be thy love, and thy love's use their treasure.

Vide REMARKS, pp. 26, 66, 92 : also Sonnets 21, 32, 36, 39, 44, 52, 53, 59, 82, 104, 106.

XXI.

So is it not with me as with that Muse
Stirr'd by a painted beauty to his verse,
Who heaven itself for ornament doth use,
And every fair with his fair doth rehearse;
Making a couplement of proud compare,
With sun and moon, with earth and sea's rich gems,
With April's firstborn flowers, and all things rare
That heaven's air in this huge rondure hems.
O, let me, true in love, but truly write,
And then believe me, my love is as fair
As any mother's child, though not so bright
As those gold candles fix'd in heaven's air:
    Let them say more that like of hearsay well;
    I will not praise, that purpose not to sell.

Vide REMARKS, pp. 68, 73, 92 : also Sonnets 20, 69, 84, 105, 144.

XXII.

My glass shall not persuade me I am old,
So long as youth and thou are of one date;
But when in thee time's furrows I behold,
Then look I death my days should expiate.
For all that beauty that doth cover thee,
Is but the seemly raiment of my heart,
Which in thy breast doth live, as thine in me:
How can I, then, be elder than thou art?
O, therefore, love, be of thyself so wary,
As I, not for myself, but for thee will;
Bearing thy heart, which I will keep so chary
As tender nurse her babe from faring ill.

  Presume not on thy heart when mine is slain;
  Thou gav'st me thine, not to give back again.

Vide REMARKS, pp. 25, 92 : also Sonnets 24, 27, 87, 102, 108.

XXIII.

As an unperfect actor on the stage,
Who with his fear is put besides his part,
Or some fierce thing replete with too much rage,
Whose strength's abundance weakens his own heart;
So I, for fear of trust, forget to say
The perfect ceremony of love's rite,
And in mine own love's strength seem to decay,
O'ercharg'd with burden of mine own love's might.
O, let my books be, then, the eloquence
And dumb presagers of my speaking breast;
Who plead for love, and look for recompence,
More than that tongue that more hath more express'd.

    O, learn to read what silent love hath writ:
    To hear with eyes belongs to love's fine wit.

Vide Sonnet 80.

XXIV.

Mine eye hath play'd the painter, and hath stel'd
Thy beauty's form in table of my heart;
My body is the frame wherein 'tis held,
And perspective it is best painter's art.
For through the painter must you see his skill,
To find where your true image pictur'd lies;
Which in my bosom's shop is hanging still,
That hath his windows glazed with thine eyes.
Now see what good turns eyes for eyes have done:
Mine eyes have drawn thy shape, and thine for me
Are windows to my breast, where-through the sun
Delights to peep, to gaze therein on thee;
   Yet eyes this cunning want to grace their art,
   They draw but what they see, know not the heart.

Vide REMARKS, p. 92 : also Sonnets 22, 27, 48, 84, 122, 153, 154.

XXV.

Let those who are in favour with their stars,
Of public honour and proud titles boast,
Whilst I, whom fortune of such triumph bars,
Unlook'd for joy in that I honour most.
Great princes' favourites their fair leaves spread
But as the marigold at the sun's eye;
And in themselves their pride lies buried,
For at a frown they in their glory die.
The painful warrior famoused for fight,
After a thousand victories once foil'd,
Is from the book of honour razed quite,
And all the rest forgot for which he toil'd:
    Then happy I, that love and am belov'd,
    Where I may not remove, nor be remov'd.

Vide REMARKS, p. 90 : also Sonnet 39.

6*

XXVI.

Lord of my love, to whom in vassalage
Thy merit hath my duty strongly knit,
To thee I send this written embassage,
To witness duty, not to show my wit:
Duty so great, which wit so poor as mine
May make seem bare, in wanting words to show it,
But that I hope some good conceit of thine
In thy soul's thought, all naked, will bestow it;
Till whatsoever star that guides my moving,
Points on me graciously with fair aspect,
And puts apparel on my tatter'd loving,
To show me worthy of thy sweet respect:
    Then may I dare to boast how I do love thee;
    Till then, not show my head where thou mayst prove me.

Vide REMARKS, p. 93: also Sonnets 16, 78, 84, 125.

XXVII.

Weary with toil, I haste me to my bed,
The dear repose for limbs with travail tir'd;
But then begins a journey in my head,
To work my mind, when body's work 's expir'd:
For then my thoughts (from far where I abide)
Intend a zealous pilgrimage to thee,
And keep my drooping eyelids open wide,
Looking on darkness which the blind do see:
Save that my soul's imaginary sight
Presents thy shadow to my sightless view,
Which, like a jewel hung in ghastly night,
Makes black night beauteous, and 'her old face new.
　　Lo, thus, by day my limbs, by night my mind,
　　For thee and for myself no quiet find.

Vide REMARKS, pp. 81, 93 : also Sonnets 22, 24, 43, 61, 113, 131, 150.

XXVIII.

How can I, then, return in happy plight,
That am debarr'd the benefit of rest?
When day's oppression is not eas'd by night,
But day by night, and night by day, oppress'd?
And each, though enemies to either's reign,
Do in consent shake hands to torture me;
The one by toil, the other to complain
How far I toil, still farther off from thee.
I tell the day, to please him, thou art bright,
And dost him grace when clouds do blot the heaven:
So flatter I the swart-complexion'd night;
When sparkling stars twire not, thou gild'st the even.

　　But day doth daily draw my sorrows longer,
　　　And night doth nightly make grief's length seem
　　　stronger.

Vide REMARKS, p. 93.

XXIX.

When in disgrace with fortune and men's eyes,
I all alone beweep my outcast state,
And trouble deaf Heaven with my bootless cries,
And look upon myself, and curse my fate,
Wishing me like to one more rich in hope,
Featur'd like him, like him with friends possess'd,
Desiring this man's art, and that man's scope,
With what I most enjoy contented least;
Yet in these thoughts myself almost despising,
Haply I think on thee,—and then my state
(Like to the lark at break of day arising
From sullen earth) sings hymns at heaven's gate;

    For thy sweet love remember'd such wealth brings,
    That then I scorn to change my state with kings.

Vide REMARKS, p. 83.

XXX.

When to the sessions of sweet silent thought
I summon up remembrance of things past,
I sigh the lack of many a thing I sought,
And with old woes new wail my dear time's waste:
Then can I drown an eye, unus'd to flow,
For precious friends hid in death's dateless night,
And weep afresh love's long-since cancell'd woe,
And moan the expense of many a vanish'd sight:
Then can I grieve at grievances foregone,
And heavily from woe to woe tell o'er
The sad account of fore-bemoaned moan,
Which I new pay as if not paid before.

But if the while I think on thee, dear friend,
All losses are restor'd, and sorrows end.

Vide REMARKS, p. 83.

XXXI.

Thy bosom is endeared with all hearts,
Which I by lacking have supposed dead;
And there reigns love, and all love's loving parts,
And all those friends which I thought buried.
How many a holy and obsequious tear
Hath dear religious love stol'n from mine eye,
As interest of the dead, which now appear
But things remov'd, that hidden in thee lie!
Thou art the grave where buried love doth live,
Hung with the trophies of my lovers gone,
Who all their parts of me to thee did give;
That due of many now is thine alone:
    Their images I lov'd I view in thee,
    And thou, all they, hast all the all of me.

Vide REMARKS, p. 83; also Sonnets 62, 112.

XXXII.

If thou survive my well-contented day,
When that churl Death my bones with dust shall cover,
And shalt by fortune once more re-survey
These poor rude lines of thy deceased lover,—
Compare them with the bettering of the time;
And though they be outstripp'd by every pen,
Reserve them for my love, not for their rhyme,
Exceeded by the height of happier men.
O, then vouchsafe me but this loving thought,—
" Had my friend's muse grown with this growing age,
A dearer birth than this his love had brought,
To march in ranks of better equipage:
    But since he died, and poets better prove,
      Theirs for their style I 'll read, his for his love."

Vide REMARKS, p. 30: also Sonnets 82, 85.

XXXIII.

Full many a glorious morning have I seen
Flatter the mountain-tops with sovereign eye,
Kissing with golden face the meadows green,
Gilding pale streams with heavenly alchemy;
Anon permit the basest clouds to ride
With ugly rack on his celestial face,
And from the forlorn world his visage hide,
Stealing unseen to west with this disgrace:
Even so my sun one early morn did shine
With all triumphant splendour on my brow;
But, out, alack! he was but one hour mine,
The region cloud hath mask'd him from me now.

    Yet him for this my love no whit disdaineth;
    Suns of the world may stain, when heaven's sun staineth.

Vide REMARKS, p. 93 : also Sonnets 75, 87.

XXXIV.

Why didst thou promise such a beauteous day,
And make me travel forth without my cloak,
To let base clouds o'ertake me in my way,
Hiding thy bravery in their rotten smoke?
'T is not enough that through the cloud thou break,
To dry the rain on my storm-beaten face,
For no man well of such a salve can speak,
That heals the wound, and cures not the disgrace:
Nor can thy shame give physic to my grief;
Though thou repent, yet I have still the loss:
The offender's sorrow lends but weak relief
To him that bears the strong offence's cross.

    Ah, but those tears are pearl which thy love sheds,
    And they are rich, and ransom all ill deeds.

XXXV.

No more be griev'd at that which thou hast done:
Roses have thorns, and silver fountains mud;
Clouds and eclipses stain both moon and sun,
And loathsome canker lives in sweetest bud.
All men make faults, and even I in this,
Authorising thy trespass with compare,
Myself corrupting, salving thy amiss,
Excusing thy sins more than thy sins are:
For to thy sensual fault I bring in sense,—
Thy adverse party is thy advocate,—
And 'gainst myself a lawful plea commence:
Such civil war is in my love and hate,
    That I an accessary needs must be
    To that sweet thief which sourly robs from me.

XXXVI.

Let me confess that we two must be twain,
Although our undivided loves are one:
So shall those blots that do with me remain,
Without thy help, by me be borne alone.
In our two loves there is but one respect,
Though in our lives a separable spite,
Which though it alter not love's sole effect,
Yet doth it steal sweet hours from love's delight.
I may not evermore acknowledge thee,
Lest my bewailed guilt should do thee shame;
Nor thou with public kindness honour me,
Unless thou take that honour from thy name:
    But do not so; I love thee in such sort,
    As, thou being mine, mine is thy good report.

Vide REMARKS, pp. 26, 74, 93: also Sonnets 20, 44, 72, 88, 89.

XXXVII.

As a decrepit father takes delight
To see his active child do deeds of youth,
So I, made lame by fortune's dearest spite,
Take all my comfort of thy worth and truth;
For whether beauty, birth, or wealth, or wit,
Or any of these all, or all, or more,
Entitled in thy parts do crowned sit,
I make my love engrafted to this store:
So then I am not lame, poor, nor despis'd,
Whilst that this shadow doth such substance give,
That I in thy abundance am suffic'd,
And by a part of all thy glory live.

    Look, what is best, that best I wish in thee:
    This wish I have: then ten times happy me!

Vide Sonnets 29, 30, 31, 53, 91.

XXXVIII.

How can my Muse want subject to invent,
While thou dost breathe, that pour'st into my verse
Thine own sweet argument, too excellent
For every vulgar paper to rehearse?
O, give thyself the thanks, if aught in me
Worthy perusal stand against thy sight;
For who's so dumb that cannot write to thee,
When thou thyself dost give invention light?
Be thou the tenth Muse, ten times more in worth
Than those old nine which rhymers invocate;
And he that calls on thee, let him bring forth
Eternal numbers to outlive long date.

 If my slight Muse do please these curious days,
  The pain be mine, but thine shall be the praise.

Vide Sonnets 14, 16, 78.

XXXIX.

. O, how thy worth with manners may I sing,
When thou art all the better part of me?
What can mine own praise to mine own self bring?
And what is 't but mine own, when I praise thee?
Even for this let us divided live,
And our dear love lose name of single one,
That by this separation I may give
That due to thee, which thou deserv'st alone.
O absence, what a torment wouldst thou prove,
Were it not thy sour leisure gave sweet leave
To entertain the time with thoughts of love,—
Which time and thoughts so sweetly doth deceive,—

> And that thou teachest how to make one twain,
> By praising him here, who doth hence remain!

Vide REMARKS, pp. 24, 74 : also Sonnets 42, 47, 62, 74, 109, 134.

XL.

Take all my loves, my love, yea, take them all;
What hast thou then more than thou hadst before?
No love, my love, that thou may'st true love call;
All mine was thine before thou hadst this more.
Then, if for my love thou my love receivest,
I cannot blame thee for my love thou usest;
But yet be blam'd, if thou thyself deceivest
By wilful taste of what thyself refusest.
I do forgive thy robbery, gentle thief,
Although thou steal thee all my poverty;
And yet, love knows, it is a greater grief
To bear love's wrong, than hate's known injury.
    Lascivious grace, in whom all ill well shows,
    Kill me with spites; yet we must not be foes.

Vide Sonnets 67, 135, 136, 142.

XLI.

Those pretty wrongs that liberty commits
When I am sometime absent from thy heart,
Thy beauty and thy years full well befits,
For still temptation follows where thou art.
Gentle thou art, and therefore to be won,
Beauteous thou art, therefore to be assail'd;
And when a woman woos, what woman's son
Will sourly leave her till she have prevail'd?
Ah me! but yet thou mightst my sweet forbear,
And chide thy beauty and thy straying youth,
Who lead thee in their riot even there
Where thou art forc'd to break a two-fold truth,—
  Hers, by thy beauty tempting her to thee,
  Thine, by thy beauty being false to me.

Vide REMARKS, p. 49 · also Sonnets 88, 139, 152.

XLII.

That thou hast her, it is not all my grief,
And yet it may be said I lov'd her dearly;
That she hath thee, is of my wailing chief,
A loss in love that touches me more nearly.
Loving offenders, thus I will excuse ye:—
Thou dost love her, because thou know'st I love her;
And for my sake even so doth she abuse me,
Suffering my friend for my sake to approve her.
If I lose thee, my loss is my love's gain,
And, losing her, my friend hath found that loss;
Both find each other, and I lose both twain,
And both for my sake lay on me this cross:
    But here's the joy,—my friend and I are one;
    Sweet flattery!—then she loves but me alone.

Vide REMARKS, pp. 41, 43 : also Sonnets 39, 47, 74, 134, 144, 147.

XLIII.

When most I wink, then do mine eyes best see,
For all the day they view things unrespected;
But when I sleep, in dreams they look on thee,
And, darkly bright, are bright in dark directed.
Then thou, whose shadow shadows doth make bright,
How would thy shadow's form form happy show
To the clear day with thy much clearer light,
When to unseeing eyes thy shade shines so!
How would, I say, mine eyes be blessed made
By looking on thee in the living day,
When in dead night thy fair imperfect shade
Through heavy sleep on sightless eyes doth stay!
　　All days are nights to see, till I see thee,
　　And nights bright days, when dreams do show thee me.

Vide Sonnets 27, 53, 61.

XLIV.

If the dull substance of my flesh were thought,
Injurious distance should not stop my way;
For then, despite of space, I would be brought,
From limits far remote, where thou dost stay.
No matter then, although my foot did stand
Upon the farthest earth remov'd from thee;
For nimble thought can jump both sea and land,
As soon as think the place where he would be.
But, ah, thought kills me, that I am not thought,
To leap large lengths of miles when thou art gone,
But that, so much of earth and water wrought,
I must attend time's leisure with my moan;
 Receiving naught by elements so slow
 But heavy tears, badges of either's woe:

Vide REMARKS, pp. 25, 92 : also Sonnets 20, 36, 52, 67, 98.

XLV.

The other two, light air and purging fire,
. Are both with thee, wherever I abide;
The first my thought, the other my desire,
These present-absent with swift motion slide.
For when these quicker elements are gone
In tender embassy of love to thee,
My life, being made of four, with two alone
Sinks down to death, oppress'd with melancholy;
Until life's composition be recur'd
By those swift messengers return'd from thee,
Who even but now come back again, assur'd
Of thy fair health, recounting it to me:

    This told, I joy; but then no longer glad,
    I send them back again, and straight grow sad

Vide Sonnet 51.

XLVI.

Mine eye and heart are at a mortal war,
How to divide the conquest of thy sight;
Mine eye my heart thy picture's sight would bar,
My heart mine eye the freedom of that right.
My heart doth plead that thou in him dost lie,—
A closet never pierc'd with crystal eyes,—
But the defendant doth that plea deny,
And says in him thy fair appearance lies.
To 'cide this title is impannelled
A quest of thoughts, all tenants to the heart;
And by their verdict is determined
The clear eye's moiety, and the dear heart's part:
  As thus,—mine eye's due is thine outward part,
  And my heart's right thine inward love of heart.

Vide REMARKS, p. 93 : also Sonnet 24.

XLVII.

Betwixt mine eye and heart a league is took,
And each doth good turns now unto the other:
When that mine eye is famish'd for a look,
Or heart in love with sighs himself doth smother,
With my love's picture then my eye doth feast,
And to the painted banquet bids my heart;
Another time mine eye is my heart's guest,
And in his thoughts of love doth share a part:
So, either by thy picture or my love,
Thyself away art present still with me;
For thou not farther than my thoughts canst move,
And I am still with them, and they with thee;
    Or, if they sleep, thy picture in my sight
    Awakes my heart to heart's and eye's delight.

Vide Sonnets 24, 39, 42, 74, 147.

XLVIII.

How careful was I when I took my way,
Each trifle under truest bars to thrust,
That to my use it might unused stay
From hands of falsehood, in sure wards of trust!
But thou, to whom my jewels trifles are,
Most worthy comfort, now my greatest grief,
Thou, best of dearest, and mine only care,
Art left the prey of every vulgar thief.
Thee have I not lock'd up in any chest,
Save where thou art not, though I feel thou art,
Within the gentle closure of my breast,
From whence at pleasure thou may'st come and part;
    And even thence thou wilt be stolen I fear,
    For truth proves thievish for a prize so dear.

Vide REMARKS, p. 69 : also Sonnet 24.

XLIX.

Against that time, if ever that time come,
When I shall see thee frown on my defects,
Whenas thy love hath cast his utmost sum,
Call'd to that audit by advis'd respects;
Against that time when thou shalt strangely pass,
And scarcely greet me with that sun, thine eye,
When love, converted from the thing it was,
Shall reasons find of settled gravity,—
Against that time do I ensconce me here
Within the knowledge of mine own desert,
And this my hand against myself uprear,
To guard the lawful reasons on thy part:
    To leave poor me thou hast the strength of laws,
    Since, why to love, I can allege no cause.

Vide Sonnets 14, 15, 32, 63.

L.

How heavy do I journey on the way,
When what I seek,—my weary travel's end,—
Doth teach that ease and that repose to say,
"Thus far the miles are measur'd from thy friend!"
The beast that bears me, tired with my woe,
Plods dully on, to bear that weight in me,
As if by some instinct the wretch did know
His rider lov'd not speed, being made from thee:
The bloody spur cannot provoke him on
That sometimes anger thrusts into his hide;
Which heavily he answers with a groan,
More sharp to me than spurring to his side;

    For that same groan doth put this in my mind,
    My grief lies onward, and my joy behind.

Vide REMARKS, p. 93.

LI.

Thus can my love excuse the slow offence
Of my dull bearer, when from thee I speed:
From where thou art why should I haste me thence?
Till I return, of posting is no need.
O, what excuse will my poor beast then find,
When swift extremity can seem but slow?
Then should I spur, though mounted on the wind,
In winged speed no motion shall I know:
Then can no horse with my desire keep pace;
Therefore desire, of perfect love being made,
Shall neigh (no dull flesh) in his fiery race;
But love, for love, thus shall excuse my jade,—
    Since from thee going he went wilful-slow,
    Towards thee I'll run, and give him leave to go.

Vide Sonnet 45.

LII.

So am I as the rich, whose blessed key
Can bring him to his sweet up-locked treasure,
The which he will not every hour survey,
For blunting the fine point of seldom pleasure.
Therefore are feasts so solemn and so rare,
Since, seldom coming, in the long year set,
Like stones of worth they thinly placed are,
Or captain jewels in the carkanet.
So is the time that keeps you, as my chest,
Or as the wardrobe which the robe doth hide,
To make some special instant special-blest,
By new unfolding his imprison'd pride.
    Blessed are you, whose worthiness gives scope,
    Being had, to triumph, being lack'd, to hope.

Vide REMARKS, p. 66 : also Sonnets 20, 44, 75, 77, 102, 125.

LIII.

What is your substance, whereof are you made,
That millions of strange shadows on you tend？
Since every one hath, every one, one shade,
And you, but one, can every shadow lend.
Describe Adonis, and the counterfeit
Is poorly imitated after you;
On Helen's cheek all art of beauty set,
And you in Grecian tires are painted new:
Speak of the spring, and foison of the year;
The one doth shadow of your beauty show,
The other as your bounty doth appear;
And you in every blessed shape we know.

    In all external grace you have some part,
    But you like none, none you, for constant heart.

Vide REMARKS, p. 44: also Sonnets 18, 20, 38, 43, 61, 92, 98, 99.

LIV.

O, how much more doth beauty beauteous seem,
By that sweet ornament which truth doth give!
The rose looks fair, but fairer we it deem
For that sweet odour which doth in it live.
The canker-blooms have full as deep a dye
As the perfumed tincture of the roses,
Hang on such thorns, and play as wantonly
When summer's breath their masked buds discloses:
But, for their virtue only is their show,
They live unwoo'd, and unrespected fade;
Die to themselves. Sweet roses do not so;
Of their sweet deaths are sweetest odours made:
    And so of you, beauteous and lovely youth,
    When that shall fade, my verse distils your truth.

Vide Sonnets 5, 6, 11, 14.

LV.

Not marble, nor the gilded monuments
Of princes, shall outlive this powerful rhyme;
But you shall shine more bright in these contents
Than unswept stone, besmear'd with sluttish time.
When wasteful war shall statues overturn,
And broils root out the work of masonry,
Nor Mars his sword nor war's quick fire shall burn
The living record of your memory.
'Gainst death and all-oblivious enmity
Shall you pace forth; your praise shall still find room,
Even in the eyes of all posterity
That wear this world out to the ending doom.
　　So, till the judgment that yourself arise,
　　You live in this, and dwell in lovers' eyes.

Vide Sonnets 7, 101.

LVI.

Sweet love, renew thy force; be it not said,
Thy edge should blunter be than appetite,
Which but to-day by feeding is allay'd,
To-morrow sharpen'd in his former might:
So, love, be thou; although to-day thou fill
Thy hungry eyes, even till they wink with fullness,
To-morrow see again, and do not kill
The spirit of love with a perpetual dullness.
Let this sad interim like the ocean be
Which parts the shore, where two contracted new
Come daily to the banks, that, when they see
Return of love, more blest may be the view;

    Or call it winter, which, being full of care,
    Makes summer's welcome thrice more wish'd, more rare.

Vide REMARKS, p. 93 : also Sonnets 111, 134.

LVII.

Being your slave, what should I do but tend
Upon the hours and times of your desire?
I have no precious time at all to spend,
Nor services to do, till you require.
Nor dare I chide the world-without-end hour,
Whilst I, my sovereign, watch the clock for you,
Nor think the bitterness of absence sour,
When you have bid your servant once adieu;
Nor dare I question with my jealous thought
Where you may be, or your affairs suppose,
But, like a sad slave, stay and think of naught,
Save, where you are, how happy you make those.
   So true a fool is love, that in your will,
   Though you do anything, he thinks no ill.

Vide Sonnets 57, 87, 150.

LVIII.

That God forbid, that made me first your slave,
I should in thought control your times of pleasure,
Or at your hand the account of hours to crave,
Being your vassal, bound to stay your leisure!
O, let me suffer, being at your beck,
The imprison'd absence of your liberty;
And patience, tame to sufferance, bide each check,
Without accusing you of injury.
Be where you list, your charter is so strong,
That you yourself may privilege your time
To what you will; to you it doth belong
Yourself to pardon of self-doing crime.

    I am to wait, though waiting so be hell;
    Not blame your pleasure, be it ill or well.

Vide REMARKS, p. 93: also Sonnets 57, 88, 89, 150.

LIX.

If there be nothing new, but that which is
Hath been before, how are our brains beguil'd,
Which, labouring for invention, bear amiss
The second burden of a former child!
O, that record could with a backward look,
Even of five hundred courses of the sun,
Show me your image in some antique book,
Since mind at first in character was done!
That I might see what the old world could say
To this composed wonder of your frame;
Whether we are mended, or whe'r better they,
Or whether revolution be the same.

    O, sure I am, the wits of former days
    To subjects worse have given admiring praise.

Vide REMARKS, p. 28 : also Sonnets 8, 32, 59, 68, 78, 106, 108.

LX.

Like as the waves make towards the pebbled shore,
So do our minutes hasten to their end;
Each changing place with that which goes before,
In sequent toil all forwards do contend.
Nativity, once in the main of light,
Crawls to maturity, wherewith being crown'd,
Crooked eclipses 'gainst his glory fight,
And Time, that gave, doth now his gift confound.
Time doth transfix the flourish set on youth,
And delves the parallels in beauty's brow;
Feeds on the rarities of nature's truth,
And nothing stands but for his scythe to mow:
    And yet, to times in hope my verse shall stand,
    Praising thy worth, despite his cruel hand.

Vide Sonnets 9, 18.

LXI.

Is it thy will thy image should keep open
My heavy eyelids to the weary night?
Dost thou desire my slumbers should be broken,
While shadows, like to thee, do mock my sight?
Is it thy spirit that thou send'st from thee
So far from home, into my deeds to pry;
To find out shames and idle hours in me,
The scope and tenor of thy jealousy?
O, no! thy love, though much, is not so great:
It is my love that keeps mine eye awake;
Mine own true love that doth my rest defeat,
To play the watchman ever for thy sake:

    For thee watch I, whilst thou dost wake elsewhere,
    From me far off, with others all too near.

Vide REMARKS, p. 81 : also Sonnets 27, 43, 53.

LXII.

Sin of self-love possesseth all mine eye,
And all my soul, and all my every part;
And for this sin there is no remedy,
It is so grounded inward in my heart.
Methinks no face so gracious is as mine,
No shape so true, no truth of such account;
And for myself mine own worth do define,
As I all other in all worths surmount.
But when my glass shows me myself indeed,
Beated and chopp'd with tann'd antiquity,
Mine own self-love quite contrary I read;
Self so self-loving were iniquity.
  'T is thee (myself) that for myself I praise,
  Painting my age with beauty of thy days.

Vide Sonnets 31, 39, 67.

LXIII.

Against my love shall be, as I am now,
With Time's injurious hand crush'd and o'erworn;
When hours have drain'd his blood, and fill'd his brow
With lines and wrinkles; when his youthful morn
Hath travell'd on to age's steepy night;
And all those beauties, whereof now he 's king,
Are vanishing or vanish'd out of sight,
Stealing away the treasure of his spring;
For such a time do I now fortify
Against confounding age's cruel knife,
That he shall never cut from memory
My sweet love's beauty, though my lover's life:
    His beauty shall in these black lines be seen,
    And they shall live, and he in them still green.

Vide Sonnets 1-17, 49, 65, 73, 74.

LXIV.

When I have seen by Time's fell hand defac'd
The rich-proud cost of outworn buried age;
When sometime lofty towers I see down-raz'd,
And brass eternal, slave to mortal rage;
When I have seen the hungry ocean gain
Advantage on the kingdom of the shore,
And the firm soil win of the watery main,
Increasing store with loss, and loss with store;
When I have seen such interchange of state,
Or state itself confounded to decay;
Ruin hath taught me thus to ruminate,—
That Time will come and take my love away.

    This thought is as a death, which cannot choose
    But weep to have that which it fears to lose.

Vide Sonnet 5.

LXV.

Since brass, nor stone, nor earth, nor boundless sea,
But sad mortality o'ersways their power,
How with his rage shall beauty hold a plea,
Whose action is no stronger than a flower?
O, how shall summer's honey breath hold out
Against the wreckful siege of battering days,
When rocks impregnable are not so stout,
Nor gates of steel so strong, but Time decays?
O fearful meditation! where, alack,
Shall Time's best jewel from Time's chest lie hid?
Or what strong hand can hold his swift foot back?
Or who his spoil of beauty can forbid?
    O, none, unless this miracle have might,
    That in black ink my love may still shine bright.

Vide REMARKS, p. 80 · also Sonnets 12, 27, 52, 100.

LXVI.

Tir'd with all these, for restful death I cry,—
As, to behold desert a beggar born,
And needy nothing trimm'd in jollity,
And purest faith unhappily forsworn,
And gilded honour shamefully misplac'd,
And maiden virtue rudely strumpeted,
And right perfection wrongfully disgrac'd,
And strength by limping sway disabled,
And art made tongue-tied by authority,
And folly, doctor-like, controlling skill,
And simple truth miscall'd simplicity,
And captive good attending captain ill:—
   Tir'd with all these, from these would I be gone,
   Save that, to die, I leave my love alone.

Vide REMARKS, pp. 25, 88.

LXVII.

Ah, wherefore with infection should he live,
And with his presence grace impiety,
That sin by him advantage should achieve,
And lace itself with his society?
Why should false painting imitate his cheek,
And steal dead seeing of his living hue?
Why should poor beauty indirectly seek
Roses of shadow, since his rose is true?
Why should he live, now Nature bankrupt is,
Beggar'd of blood to blush through lively veins?
For she hath no exchequer now but his,
And, proud of many, lives upon his gains.

    O, him she stores, to show what wealth she had
    In days long since, before these last so bad.

Vide REMARKS, p. 94 : also Sonnets 20, 36, 40, 44, 62, 69, 95, 108, 109, 127.

LXVIII.

Thus is his cheek the map of days outworn,
When beauty liv'd and died as flowers do now,
Before these bastard signs of fair were borne,
Or durst inhabit on a living brow ;
Before the golden tresses of the dead,
The right of sepulchres, were shorn away,
To live a second life on second head ;
Ere beauty's dead fleece made another gay :
In him those holy antique hours are seen,
Without all ornament, itself, and true,
Making no summer of another's green,
Robbing no old to dress his beauty new ;
 And him as for a map doth Nature store,
 To show false Art what beauty was of yore.

Vide Sonnets 59, 106, 108, 125, 127.

LXIX.

Those parts of thee that the world's eye doth view,
Want nothing that the thought of hearts can mend;
All tongues, the voice of souls, give thee that due,
Uttering bare truth, even so as foes commend.
Thine outward thus with outward praise is crown'd;
But those same tongues, that give thee so thine own,
In other accents do this praise confound,
By seeing farther than the eye hath shown.
They look into the beauty of thy mind,
And that, in guess, they measure by thy deeds,
Then, churls, their thoughts, although their eyes were kind,
To thy fair flower add the rank smell of weeds:
    But why thy odour matcheth not thy show.
    The solve is this,—that thou dost common grow.

Vide Sonnets 21, 67, 84, 103, 152.

LXX.

That thou **art blam**'d shall not be thy defect,
For slander's mark was ever yet the fair;
The ornament of beauty is suspect,
A crow that flies in heaven's sweetest air.
So thou be good, slander doth but approve
Thy worth the greater, being woo'd of time;
For canker vice the sweetest buds doth love,
And thou present'st a pure unstained prime.
Thou hast pass'd by the ambush of young days,
Either not assail'd, or victor being charg'd;
Yet this thy praise cannot be so thy praise,
To tie up envy, evermore enlarg'd:
    If some suspect of ill mask'd not thy show,
    Then thou alone kingdoms of hearts shouldst owe.

Vide Sonnet 125.

LXXI.

No longer mourn for me when I am dead,
Than you shall hear the surly sullen bell
Give warning to the world that I am fled
From this vile world, with vilest worms to dwell:
Nay, if you read this line, remember not
The hand that writ it; for I love you so,
That I in your sweet thoughts would be forgot,
If thinking on me then should make you woe.
O, if, I say, you look upon this verse,
When I perhaps compounded am with clay,
Do not so much as my poor name rehearse;
But let your love even with my life decay;

    Lest the wise world should look into your moan,
    And mock you with me after I am gone.

Vide Sonnet 64.

LXXII.

O, lest the world should task you to recite
What merit liv'd in me, that you should love
After my death,—dear love, forget me quite,
For you in me can nothing worthy prove;
Unless you would devise some virtuous lie,
To do more for me than mine own desert,
And hang more praise upon deceased I
Than niggard truth would willingly impart:
O, lest your true love may seem false in this,
That you for love speak well of me untrue,
My name be buried where my body is,
And live no more to shame nor me nor you.

    For I am sham'd by that which I bring forth,
    And so should you, ·to love things nothing worth.

Vide Sonnets 36, 48, 78, 89.

LXXIII.

That time of year thou may'st in me behold
When yellow leaves, or none, or few, do hang
Upon those boughs which shake against, the cold,
Bare ruin'd choirs, where late the sweet birds sang.
In me thou seest the twilight of such day
As after sunset fadeth in the west;
Which by and by black night doth take away,
Death's second self, that seals up all in rest.
In me thou seest the glowing of such fire,
That on the ashes of his youth doth lie,
As the death-bed whereon it must expire,
Consum'd with that which it was nourish'd by.
    This thou perceiv'st, which makes thy love more strong,
    To love that well which thou must leave ere long:

Vide Sonnet 63.

8*

LXXIV.

But be contented: when that fell arrest
Without all bail shall carry me away,
My life hath in this line some interest,
Which for memorial still with thee shall stay.
When thou reviewest this, thou dost review
The very part was consecrate to thee:
The earth can have but earth, which is his due;
My spirit is thine, the better part of me:
So, then, thou hast but lost the dregs of life,
The prey of worms, my body being dead;
The coward conquest of a wretch's knife,
Too base of thee to be remembered.

    The worth of that, is that which it contains,
    And that is this, and this with thee remains.

Vide REMARKS, pp. 24, 90: also Sonnets 5, 6, 9, 10, 13, 42, 47, 61, 62, 63, 81, 108

LXXV.

So are you to my thoughts, as food to life,
Or as sweet-season'd showers are to the ground;
And for the peace of you I hold such strife
As 'twixt a miser and his wealth is found;
Now proud as an enjoyer, and anon
Doubting the filching age will steal his treasure,
Now counting best to be. with you alone,
Then better'd that the world may see my pleasure:
Sometime all full with feasting on your sight,
And by and by clean starved for a look;
Possessing or pursuing no delight,
Save what is had or must from you be took.
    Thus do I pine and surfeit day by day,
    Or gluttoning on all, or all away.

Vide REMARKS, p. 67 : also Sonnets 33, 52, 77, 87.

LXXVI.

Why is my verse so barren of new pride,
So far from variation or quick change?
Why, with the time, do I not glance aside
To new-found methods and to compounds strange?
Why write I still all one, ever the same,
And keep invention in a noted weed,
That every word doth almost tell my name,
Showing their birth, and where they did proceed?
O, know, sweet love, I always write of you,
And you and love are still my argument;
So all my best is dressing old words new,
Spending again what is already spent:

    For as the sun is daily new and old,
    So is my love still telling what is told.

Vide Sonnets 105, 108.

LXXVII.

Thy glass will show thee how thy beauties wear,
Thy dial how thy precious minutes waste;
The vacant leaves thy mind's imprint will bear,
And of this book this learning may'st thou taste.
The wrinkles which thy glass will truly show,
Of mouthed graves will give thee memory;
Thou by thy dial's shady stealth may'st know
Time's thievish progress to eternity.
Look, what thy memory cannot contain,
Commit to these waste blanks, and thou shalt find
Those children nurs'd, deliver'd from thy brain,
To take a new acquaintance of thy mind.
    These offices, so oft as thou wilt look,
    Shall profit thee, and much enrich thy book.

Vide REMARKS, p. 68 : also Sonnets 1, 3, 52, 75, 122.

LXXVIII.

So oft have I invok'd thee for my Muse,
And found such fair assistance in my verse,
As every alien pen hath got my use,
And under thee their poesy disperse.
Thine eyes, that taught the dumb on high to sing,
And heavy ignorance aloft to fly,
Have added feathers to the learned's wing,
And given grace a double majesty.
Yet be most proud of that which I compile,
Whose influence is thine, and born of thee:
In others' works thou dost but mend the style,
And arts with thy sweet graces graced be;

    But thou art all my art, and dost advance
    As high as learning my rude ignorance.

Vide REMARKS, pp. 21, 80 : also Sonnets 1-17, 26, 72, 79, 125, 127.

LXXIX.

Whilst I alone did call upon thy aid,
My verse alone had all thy gentle grace;
But now my gracious numbers are decay'd,
And my sick muse doth give another place.
I grant, sweet love, thy lovely argument
Deserves the travail of a worthier pen;
Yet what of thee thy poet doth invent,
He robs thee of, and pays it thee again.
He lends thee virtue, and he stole that word
From thy behaviour; beauty doth he give,
And found it in thy cheek; he can afford
No praise to thee but what in thee doth live.
    Then thank him not for that which he doth say,
    Since what he owes thee thou thyself dost pay.

Vide Sonnets 16, 78, 80.

LXXX.

O, how I faint when I of you do write,
Knowing a better spirit doth use your name,
And in the praise thereof spends all his might,
To make me tongue-tied, speaking of your fame!
But since your worth, wide as the ocean is,
The humble as the proudest sail doth bear,
My saucy bark, inferior far to his,
On your broad main doth wilfully appear.
Your shallowest help will hold me up afloat,
Whilst he upon your soundless deep doth ride;
Or, being wreck'd, I am a worthless boat,
He of tall building, and of goodly pride:
    Then if he thrive, and I be cast away,
    The worst was this,—my love was my decay.

Vide Sonnets 23, 79, 86, 141.

LXXXI.

Or I shall live your epitaph to make,
Or you survive when I in earth am rotten;
From hence your memory death cannot take,
Although in me each part will be forgotten.
Your name from hence immortal life shall have,
Though I, once gone, to all the world must die:
The earth can yield me but a common grave,
When you entombed in men's eyes shall lie.
Your monument shall be my gentle verse,
Which eyes not yet created shall o'er-read;
And tongues to be, your being shall rehearse,
When all the breathers of this world are dead;
   You still shall live (such virtue hath my pen)
   Where breath most breathes,—even in the mouths of men.

Vide Sonnets 18, 74.

LXXXII.

I grant thou wert not married to my Muse,
And therefore may'st without attaint o'erlook
The dedicated words which writers use
Of their fair subject, blessing every book.
Thou art as fair in knowledge as in hue,
Finding thy worth a limit past my praise;
And therefore art enforc'd to seek anew
Some fresher stamp of the time-bettering days.
And do so, love; yet when they have devis'd
What strained touches rhetoric can lend,
Thou, truly fair, wert truly sympathiz'd
In true plain words by thy true-telling friend;
    And their gross painting might be better us'd
    Where cheeks need blood,—in thee it is abus'd.

Vide Sonnets 15, 16, 20, 28, 32, 103.

LXXXIII.

I never saw that you did painting need,
And therefore to your fair no painting set;
I found, or thought I found, you did exceed
The barren tender of a poet's debt:
And therefore have' I slept in your report,
That you yourself, being extant, well might show
How far a modern quill doth come too short,
Speaking of worth, what worth in you doth grow.
This silence for my sin you did impute,
Which shall be most my glory, being dumb;
For I impair not beauty, being mute,
When others would give life, and bring a tomb.

    There lives more life in one of your fair eyes,
    Than both your poets can in praise devise.

Vide REMARKS, p. 32 : also Sonnets 17, 19, 32, 59, 84, 106, 109.

LXXXIV.

Who is it that says most? which can say more
Than this rich praise,—that you alone are you?
In whose confine immured is the store
Which should example where your equal grew.
Lean penury within that pen doth dwell,
That to his subject lends not some small glory;
But he that writes of you, if he can tell
That you are you, so dignifies his story,
Let him but copy what in you is writ,
Not making worse what nature made so clear,
And such a counterpart shall fame his wit,
Making his style admired everywhere.

  You to your beauteous blessings add a curse,
  Being fond on praise, which makes your praises worse.

Vide Sonnets 16, 21, 24, 26, 69, 83, 103, 109.

LXXXV.

My tongue-tied Muse in manners holds her still,
While comments of your praise, richly compil'd,
Reserve their character with golden quill,
And precious phrase by all the muses fil'd.
I think good thoughts, while others write good words,
And, like unletter'd clerk, still cry "Amen"
To every hymn that able spirit affords,
In polish'd form of well-refined pen.
Hearing you prais'd, I say, "'T is so, 't is true,"
And to the most of praise add something more;
But that is in my thought, whose love to you,
Though words come hindmost, holds his rank before.
    Then others for the breath of words respect,—
    Me for my dumb thoughts, speaking in effect.

Vide REMARKS, p. 15 : also Sonnet 32.

LXXXVI.

Was it the proud full sail of his great verse,
Bound for the prize of all-too-precious you,
That did my ripe thoughts in my brain inherse,
Making their tomb the womb wherein they grew?
Was it his spirit, by spirits taught to write
Above a mortal pitch, that struck me dead?
No, neither he, nor his compeers by night
Giving him aid, my verse astonished.
He, nor that affable familiar ghost
Which nightly gulls him with intelligence,
As victors, of my silence cannot boast;
I was not sick of any fear from thence:
　　But when your countenance fil'd up his line
　　Then lack'd I matter; that enfeebled mine.

Vide Sonnets 1-17, 80.

LXXXVII.

Farewell! thou art too dear for my possessing,
And like enough thou know'st thy estimate:
The charter of thy worth gives thee releasing;
My bonds in thee are all determinate.
For how do I hold thee but by thy granting?
And for that riches where is my deserving?
The cause of this fair gift in me is wanting,
And so my patent back again is swerving.
Thyself thou gav'st, thy own worth then not knowing,
Or me, to whom thou gav'st it, else mistaking;
So thy great gift, upon misprision growing,
Comes home again, on better judgment making.
 Thus have I had thee, as a dream doth flatter
 In sleep a king, but, waking, no such matter.

Vide Sonnets 22, 33, 57, 58, 75, 152.

LXXXVIII.

When thou shalt be dispos'd to set me light,
And place my merit in the eye of scorn,
Upon thy side against myself I 'll fight,
And prove thee virtuous, though thou art forsworn
With mine own weakness being best acquainted,
Upon thy part I can set down a story
Of faults conceal'd, wherein I am attainted;
That thou, in losing me, shalt win much glory:
And I by this will be a gainer too;
For bending all my loving thoughts on thee,
The injuries that to myself I do,
Doing thee vantage, double-vantage me.
 Such is my love, to thee I so belong,
  That for thy right myself will bear all wrong.

Vide Sonnets 36, 39, 42.

LXXXIX.

Say that thou didst forsake me for some fault,
And I will comment upon that offence:
Speak of my lameness, and I straight will halt,
Against thy reasons making no defence.
Thou canst not, love, disgrace me half so ill,
To set a form upon desired change,
As I 'll myself disgrace: knowing thy will,
I will acquaintance strangle, and look strange;
Be absent from thy walks; and in my tongue
Thy sweet-beloved name no more shall dwell,
Lest I, too much profane, should do it wrong,
And haply of our old acquaintance tell.

 For thee, against myself I 'll vow debate,
 For I must ne'er love him whom thou dost hate.

Vide Sonnets 36, 58, 72, 149, 150.

9

XC.

Then hate me when thou wilt; if ever, now;
Now, while the world is bent my deeds to cross,
Join with the spite of fortune, make me bow,
And do not drop in for an after-loss:
Ah, do not, when my heart hath scap'd this sorrow,
Come in the rearward of a conquer'd woe;
Give not a windy night a rainy morrow,
To linger out a purpos'd overthrow.
If thou wilt leave me, do not leave me last,
When other petty griefs have done their spite,
But in the onset come: so shall I taste
At first the very worst of fortune's might;
        And other strains of woe, which now seem woe,
        Compar'd with loss of thee will not seem so.

XCI.

Some glory in their birth, some in their skill,
Some in their wealth, some in their body's force;
Some in their garments, though new-fangled ill;
Some in their hawks and hounds, some in their horse;
And every humour hath his adjunct pleasure,
Wherein it finds a joy above the rest:
But these particulars are not my measure;
All these I better in one general best.
Thy love is better than high birth to me,
Richer than wealth, prouder than garments' cost,
Of more delight than hawks or horses be;
And, having thee, of all men's pride I boast:
   Wretched in this alone, that thou may'st take
   All this away, and me most wretched make.

Vide REMARKS, p. 90 : also Sonnets 29, 30, 31, 37, 92.

XCII.

But do thy worst to steal thyself away,
For term of life thou art assured mine;
And life no longer than thy love will stay,
For it depends upon that love of thine.
Then need I not to fear the worst of wrongs,
When in the least of them my life hath end.
I see a better state to me belongs
Than that which on thy humour doth depend:
Thou canst not vex me with inconstant mind,
Since that my life on thy revolt doth lie.
O, what a happy title do I find,
Happy to have thy love, happy to die!
    But what's so blessed-fair that fears no blot?
    Thou may'st be false, and yet I know it not:

Vide Sonnets 53, 91, 104, 122.

XCIII.

So shall I live, supposing thou art true,
Like a deceived husband; so love's face
May still seem love to me, though alter'd new;
Thy looks with me, thy heart in other place:
For there can live no hatred in thine eye,
Therefore in that I cannot know thy change.
In many's looks the false heart's history
Is writ in moods, and frowns, and wrinkles strange;
But heaven in thy creation did decree
That in thy face sweet love should ever dwell;
Whate'er thy thoughts or thy heart's workings be,
Thy looks should nothing thence but sweetness tell.
    How like Eve's apple doth thy beauty grow,
    If thy sweet virtue answer not thy show!

Vide Sonnets 94, 138.

XCIV.

They that have power to hurt and will do none,
That do not do the thing they most do show,
Who, moving others, are themselves as stone,
Unmoved, cold, and to temptation slow;
They rightly do inherit heaven's graces,
And husband nature's riches from expense;
They are the lords and owners of their faces,
Others but stewards of their excellence.
The summer's flower is to the summer sweet,
Though to itself it only live and die;
But if that flower with base infection meet,
The basest weed outbraves his dignity:

> For sweetest things turn sourest by their deeds;
> Lilies that fester smell far worse than weeds.

Vide Sonnet 93.

XCV.

How sweet and lovely dost thou make the shame,
Which, like a canker in the fragrant rose,
Doth spot the beauty of thy budding name!
O, in what sweets dost thou thy sins enclose!
That tongue that tells the story of thy days,
Making lascivious comments on thy sport,
Cannot dispraise but in a kind of praise;
Naming thy name blesses an ill report.
O, what a mansion have those vices got
Which for their habitation chose out thee,
Where beauty's veil doth cover every blot,
And all things turn to fair, that eyes can see!
    Take heed, dear heart, of this large privilege;
    The hardest knife ill-us'd doth lose his edge.

Vide Sonnets 67, 96, 150.

XCVI.

Some say, thy fault is youth, some wantonness;
Some say, thy grace is youth and gentle sport;
Both grace and faults are lov'd of more and less;
Thou mak'st faults graces that to thee resort.
As on the finger of a throned queen
The basest jewel will be well esteem'd,
So are those errors that in thee are seen
To truths translated, and for true things deem'd.
How many lambs might the stern wolf betray,
If like a lamb he could his looks translate!
How many gazers might'st thou lead away,
If thou wouldst use the strength of all thy state!
    But do not so; I love thee in such sort,
      As, thou being mine, mine is thy good report.

Vide Sonnets 95, 150.

XCVII.

How like a winter hath my absence been
From thee, the pleasure of the fleeting year!
What freezings have I felt, what dark days seen!
What old December's bareness everywhere!
And yet this time remov'd was summer's time;
The teeming autumn, big with rich increase,
Bearing the wanton burden of the prime,
Like widow'd wombs after their lords' decease:
Yet this abundant issue seem'd to me
But hope of orphans, and unfather'd fruit;
For summer and his pleasures wait on thee,
And, thou away, the very birds are mute;
    Or if they sing, 't is with so dull a cheer,
    That leaves look pale, dreading the winter's near.

XCVIII.

From you have I been absent in the spring,
When proud-pied April, dress'd in all his trim,
Hath put a spirit of youth in everything,
That heavy Saturn laugh'd and leap'd with him.
Yet nor the lays of birds, nor the sweet smell
Of different flowers in odour and in hue,
Could make me any summer's story tell,
Or from their proud lap pluck them where they grew:
Nor did I wonder at the lilies white,
Nor praise the deep vermilion in the rose;
They were but sweet, but figures of delight,
Drawn after you,—you pattern of all those.

    Yet seem'd it winter still, and, you away,
    As with your shadow I with these did play:

Vide Sonnets 20, 44, 53.

XCIX.

The forward violet thus did I chide :—
Sweet thief, whence didst thou steal thy sweet that smells,
If not from my love's breath ? The purple pride,
Which on thy soft cheek for complexion dwells,
In my love's veins thou hast too grossly dy'd.
The lily I condemned for thy hand ;
And buds of marjoram had stol'n thy hair :
The roses fearfully on thorns did stand,
One blushing shame, another white despair ;
A third, nor red nor white, had stol'n of both,
And to his robbery had annex'd thy breath ;
But, for his theft, in pride of all his growth
A vengeful canker eat him up to death.
 More flowers I noted, yet I none could see,
 But sweet or colour it had stol'n from thee.

Vide Sonnet 53.

C.

Where art thou, Muse, that thou forgett'st so long
To speak of that which gives thee all thy might?
Spend'st thou thy fury on some worthless song,
Darkening thy power to lend base subjects light?
Return, forgetful Muse, and straight redeem
In gentle numbers time so idly spent;
Sing to the ear that doth thy lays esteem,
And gives thy pen both skill and argument.
Rise, resty Muse, my love's sweet face survey,
If Time have any wrinkle graven there;
If any, be a satire to decay,
And make Time's spoils despised everywhere.
    Give my love fame faster than Time wastes life;
    So thou prevent'st his scythe and crooked knife.

Vide Sonnets 65, 101.

CI.

O truant Muse, what shall be thy amends
For thy neglect of truth in beauty dy'd?
Both truth and beauty on my love depends;
So dost thou too, and therein dignified.
Make answer, Muse: wilt thou not haply say,
"Truth needs no colour, with his colour fix'd;
Beauty no pencil, beauty's truth to lay;
But best is best, if never intermix'd?"
Because he needs no praise, wilt thou be dumb?
Excuse not silence so; for 't lies in thee
To make him much outlive a gilded tomb,
And to be prais'd of ages yet to be.

 Then do thy office, Muse; I teach thee how
 To make him seem long hence as he shows now.

Vide Sonnets 15, 16, 100.

CII.

My love is strengthen'd, though more weak in **seeming**;
I love not less, though less the show appear;
That love is merchandiz'd, whose rich esteeming
The owner's tongue doth publish everywhere.
Our love was new, and then but in the spring,
When I was wont to greet it with my lays;
As Philomel in summer's front doth sing,
And stops her pipe in growth of riper days:
Not that the summer is less pleasant now
Than when her mournful hymns did hush the night,
But that wild music burdens every bough,
And sweets grown common lose their dear delights.
　　Therefore, like her, I sometime hold my tongue,
　　Because I would not dull you with my song.

Vide REMARKS, pp. 61, 68 : also Sonnets 22, 52, 75, 77, 147.

CIII.

Alack, what poverty my Muse brings forth,
That having such a scope to show her pride,
The argument, all bare, is of more worth,
Than when it hath my added praise beside!
O, blame me not, if I no more can write!
Look in your glass, and there appears a face
That over-goes my blunt invention quite,
Dulling my lines, and doing me disgrace.
Were it not sinful, then, striving to mend,
To mar the subject that before was well?
For to no other pass my verses tend,
Than of your graces and your gifts to tell;
 And more, much more, than in my verse can sit,
 Your own glass shows you, when you look in it.

Vide Sonnets 17, 69, 82, 83, 106.

CIV.

To me, fair friend, you never can be old,
For as you were when first your eye I ey'd,
Such seems your beauty still. Three winters' cold
Have from the forests shook three summers' pride,
Three beauteous springs to yellow autumn turn'd
In process of the seasons have I seen,
Three April perfumes in three hot Junes burn'd,
Since first I saw you fresh, which yet are green.
Ah, yet doth beauty, like a dial-hand,
Steal from his figure, and no pace perceiv'd;
So your sweet hue, which methinks still doth stand,
Hath motion, and mine eye may be deceiv'd:
　　For fear of which, hear this, thou age unbred,—
　　Ere you were born, was beauty's summer dead.

Vide REMARKS, p. 57 : also Sonnets 20, 92, 127.

CV.

Let not my love be call'd idolatry,
Nor my beloved as an idol show,
Since all alike my songs and praises be
To one, of one, still such, and ever so.
Kind is my love to-day, to-morrow kind,
Still constant in a wondrous excellence;
Therefore my verse, to constancy confin'd,
One thing expressing, leaves out difference.
Fair, kind, and true, is all my argument,—
Fair, kind, and true, varying to other words;
And in this change is my invention spent,
Three themes in one, which wondrous scope affords.

    Fair, kind, and true, have often liv'd alone,
    Which three, till now, never kept seat in one.

Vide Sonnets 76, 108.

CVI.

When in the chronicle of wasted time
I see descriptions of the fairest wights,
And beauty making beautiful old rhyme,
In praise of ladies dead, and lovely knights;
Then in the blazon of sweet beauty's best,
Of hand, of foot, of lip, of eye, of brow,
I see their antique pen would have express'd
Even such a · beauty as you master now.
So all their praises are but prophecies
Of this our time, all you prefiguring;
And, for they look'd but with divining eyes,
They · had not skill enough your worth to ·sing :
    For we, which now behold these present days,
    Have eyes to wonder, but lack tongues to praise.

Vide REMARKS, p. 29: also Sonnets 20, 32, 59, 68, 103.

CVII.

Not mine own fears, nor the prophetic soul
Of the wide world dreaming on things to come,
Can yet the lease of my true love control,
Suppos'd as forfeit to a confin'd doom.
The mortal moon hath her eclipse endur'd,
And the sad augurs mock their own presage;
Incertainties now crown themselves assur'd,
And peace proclaims olives of endless age.
Now with the drops of this most balmy time
My love looks fresh, and Death to me subscribes,
Since, spite of him, I 'll live in this poor rhyme,
While he insults o'er dull and speechless tribes:
 And thou in this shalt find thy monument,
 When tyrants' crests and tombs of brass are spent.

Vide Sonnet 146.

CVIII.

What 's in the brain, that ink may character,
Which hath not figur'd to thee my true spirit?
What 's new to speak, what new to register,
That may express my love, or thy dear merit?
Nothing, sweet boy; but yet, like prayers divine,
I must each day say o'er the very same;
Counting no old thing old, thou mine, I thine,
Even as when first I hallow'd thy fair name.
So that eternal love in love's fresh case
Weighs not the dust and injury of age,
Nor gives to necessary wrinkles place,
But makes antiquity for aye his page;
   Finding the first conceit of love there bred,
    Where time and outward form would show it dead.

Vide REMARKS, pp. 20, 57: also Sonnets 22, 39, 59, 67, 68, 74, 76, 105, 109.

CIX.

O, never say that I was false of heart,
Though absence seem'd my flame to qualify.
As easy might I from myself depart,
As from my soul, which in thy breast doth lie:
That is my home of love: if I have rang'd,
Like him that travels, I return again;
Just to the time, not with the time exchang'd,
So that myself bring water for my stain.
Never believe, though in my nature reign'd
All frailties that besiege all kinds of blood,
That it could so preposterously be stain'd,
To leave for nothing all thy sum of good;

 For nothing this wide universe I call,
 Save thou, my rose; in it thou art my all.

Vide Sonnets 39, 67, 83, 84, 103, 108, 112.

CX.

Alas, 'tis true I have gone here and there,
And made myself a motley to the view,
Gor'd mine own thoughts, sold cheap what is most dear,
Made old offences of affections new:
Most true it is, that I have look'd on truth
Askance and strangely: but, by all above,
These blenches gave my heart another youth,
And worse essays prov'd thee my best of love.
Now all is done, save what shall have no end:
Mine appetite I never more will grind
On newer proof, to try an older friend,
A god in love, to whom I am confin'd.
    Then give me welcome, next my heaven the best,
    Even to thy pure and most most loving breast.

Vide Sonnets 100, 117, 119.

CXI.

O, for my sake do you with Fortune chide,
The guilty goddess of my harmful deeds,
That did not better for my life provide,
Than public means, which public manners breeds.
Thence comes it that my name receives a brand;
And almost thence my nature is subdued
To what it works in, like the dyer's hand:
Pity me, then, and wish I were renew'd;
Whilst, like a willing patient, I will drink
Potions of eisel 'gainst my strong infection;
No bitterness that I will bitter think,
Nor double penance, to correct correction.

Pity me, then, dear friend, and I assure ye,
Even that your pity is enough to cure me.

Vide Sonnet 56.

CXII.

Your love and pity doth th' impression fill
Which vulgar scandal stamp'd upon my brow ;
For what care I who calls me well or ill,
So you o'ergreen my bad, my good allow?
You are my all-the-world, and I must strive
To know my shames and praises from your tongue;
None else to me, nor I to none alive,
That my steel'd sense or changes, right or wrong.
In so profound abysm I throw all care
Of others' voices, that my adder's sense
. To critic and to flatterer stopped are.
Mark how with my neglect I do dispense:—
    You are so strongly in my purpose bred,
    That all the world besides methinks are dead.

Vide Sonnets 31, 109, 121.

CXIII.

Since I left you, mine eye is in my mind;
And that which governs me to go about
Doth part his function, and is partly blind,
Seems seeing, but effectually is out;
For it no form delivers to the heart
Of bird, of flower, or shape, which it doth latch:
Of his quick objects hath the mind no part,
Nor his own vision holds what it doth catch;
For if it see the rud'st or gentlest sight,
The most sweet favour, or deformed'st creature,
The mountain or the sea, the day or night,
The crow or dove, it shapes them to your feature:
 Incapable of more, replete with you,
 My most true mind thus maketh mine untrue.

Vide Sonnets 27, 137, 148, 150.

CXIV.

Or whether doth my mind, being crown'd with you,
Drink up the monarch's plague, this flattery?
Or whether shall I say, mine eye saith true,
And that your love taught it this alchemy,
To make of monsters and things indigest
Such cherubins as your sweet self resemble,
Creating every bad a perfect best,
As fast as objects to his beams assemble?
O, 't is the first; 't is flattery in my seeing,
And my great mind most kingly drinks it up:
Mine eye well knows what with his gust is 'greeing,
And to his palate doth prepare the cup:
    If it be poison'd, 't is the lesser sin
    That mine eye loves it, and doth first begin.

CXV.

Those lines that I before have writ, do lie;
Even those that said I could not love you dearer:
Yet then my judgment knew no reason why
My most full flame should afterwards burn clearer.
But reckoning Time, whose million'd accidents
Creep in 'twixt vows, and change decrees of kings,
Tan sacred beauty, blunt the sharp'st intents,
Divert strong minds to the course of altering things;
Alas, why, fearing of Time's tyranny,
Might I not then say, "Now I love you best,"
When I was certain o'er incertainty,
Crowning the present, doubting of the rest?
   Love is a babe; then might I not say so,
   To give full growth to that which still doth grow?

CXVI.

Let me not to the marriage of true minds
Admit impediments. Love is not love
Which alters when it alteration finds,
Or bends with the remover to remove:
O, no! it is an ever-fixed mark,
That looks on tempests, and is never shaken;
It is the star to every wandering bark,
Whose worth 's unknown, although his height be taken.
Love 's not Time's fool, though rosy lips and cheeks
Within his bending sickle's compass come;
Love alters not with his brief hours and weeks,
But bears it out even to the edge of doom.
 If this be error, and upon me prov'd,
  I never writ, nor no man ever lov'd.

CXVII.

Accuse me thus:—that I have scanted all
Wherein I should your great deserts repay;
Forgot upon your dearest love to call,
Whereto all bonds do tie me day by day;
That I have frequent been with unknown minds,
And given to time your own dear-purchas'd right;
That I have hoisted sail to all the winds
Which should transport me farthest from your sight.
Book both my wilfulness and errors down,
And on just proof surmise accumulate;
Bring me within the level of your frown,
But shoot not at me in your waken'd hate;
    Since my appeal says, I did strive to prove
    The .constancy and virtue of your love.

Vide Sonnet 110.

CXVIII.

Like as, to make our appetites more keen,
With eager compounds we our palate urge;
As, to prevent our maladies unseen,
We sicken to shun sickness when we purge;
Even so, being full of your ne'er-cloying sweetness,
To bitter sauces did I frame my feeding;
And, sick of welfare, found a kind of meetness
To be diseas'd, ere that there was true needing.
Thus policy in love, to anticipate
The ills that were not, grew to faults assured,
And brought to medicine a healthful state,
Which, rank of goodness, would by ill be cured:
    But thence I learn, and find the lesson true,
    Drugs poison him that so fell sick of you.

CXIX.

What potions have I drunk of Syren tears,
Distill'd from limbecks foul as hell within,
Applying fears to hopes, and hopes to fears,
Still losing when I saw myself to win!
What wretched errors hath my heart committed,
Whilst it hath thought itself so blessed never!
How have mine eyes out of their spheres been fitted,
In the distraction of this madding fever!
O benefit of ill! now I find true
That better is by evil still made better;
And ruin'd love, when it is built anew,
Grows fairer than at first, more strong, far greater.
   So I return rebuk'd to my content,
    And gain by ill thrice more than I have spent.

Vide Sonnet 110.

CXX.

That you were once unkind befriends me now,
And for that sorrow, which I then did feel,
Needs must I under my transgression bow,
Unless my nerves were brass or hammer'd steel.
For if you were by my unkindness shaken,
As I by yours, you 've pass'd a hell of time;
And I, a tyrant, have no leisure taken
To weigh how once I suffer'd in your crime.
O, that our night of woe might have remember'd
My deepest sense, how hard true sorrow hits,
And soon to you, as you to me, then tender'd
The humble salve which wounded bosoms fits!

   But that your trespass now becomes a fee;
   Mine ransoms yours, and yours must ransom me.

Vide REMARKS, p. 70: also Sonnet 119.

CXXI.

'T is better to be vile than vile esteem'd,
When not to be, receives reproach of being;
And the just pleasure. lost, which is so deem'd
Not by our feeling, but by others' seeing:
For why should others' false adulterate eyes
Give salutation to my sportive blood?
Or on my frailties why are frailer spies,
Which in their wills count bad what I think 'good?
No,—I am that I am; and they that level
At my abuses, reckon up their own:
I may be straight, though they themselves be bevel;
By their rank thoughts my deeds must not be shown;
   Unless this general evil they maintain,—
    All men are bad, and in their badness reign.

Vide REMARKS, p. 50 : also Sonnets 111, 112.

CXXII.

Thy gift, thy tables, are within my brain
Full character'd with lasting memory,
Which shall above that idle rank remain,
Beyond all date, even to eternity :
Or, at the least, so long as brain and heart
Have faculty by nature to subsist ;
Till each to raz'd oblivion yield his part
Of thee, thy record never can be miss'd.
That poor retention could not so much hold,
Nor need I tallies thy dear love to score ;
Therefore to give them from me was I bold,
To trust those tables that receive thee more :
  To keep an adjunct to remember thee,
  Were to import forgetfulness in me.

Vide REMARKS, pp. 45, 46, 49 : also Sonnets 24, 77, 92, 153, 154.

CXXIII.

No, Time, thou shalt not boast that I do change:
Thy pyramids built up with newer might
To me are nothing novel, nothing strange;
They are but dressings of a former sight.
Our dates are brief, and therefore we admire
What thou dost foist upon us that is old;
And rather make them born to our desire,
Than think that we before have heard them told.
Thy registers and thee I both defy,
Not wondering at the present nor the past;
For thy records and what we see do lie,
Made more or less by thy continual haste.

    This I do vow, and this shall ever be,
    I will be true, despite thy scythe and thee.

Vide REMARKS, p. 50 : also Sonnets 18, 59.

CXXIV.

If my dear love were but the child of state,
It might for fortune's bastard be unfather'd,
As subject to Time's love, or to Time's hate,
Weeds among weeds, or flowers with flowers gather'd.
No, it was builded far from accident;
It suffers not in smiling pomp, nor falls
Under the blow of thralled discontent,
Whereto the inviting time our fashion calls:
It fears not policy, that heretic,
Which works on leases of short-number'd hours,
But all alone stands hugely politic,
That it nor grows with heat, nor drowns with showers.
 To this I witness call the fools of time,
  Which die for goodness, who have liv'd for crime.

CXXV.

Were 't aught to me I bore the canopy,
With my extern the outward honouring,
Or laid great bases for eternity,
Which prove more short than waste or ruining?
Have I not seen dwellers on form and favour
Lose all, and more, by paying too much rent,
For compound sweet foregoing simple savour,
Pitiful thrivers, in their gazing spent?
No, let me be obsequious in thy · heart,
And take thou my oblation, poor but free,
Which is not mix'd with seconds, knows no art,
But mutual render, only me for thee.

  Hence, thou suborn'd informer! a true soul,
  When most impeach'd, stands least in thy control.

Vide REMARKS, p. 94 : also Sonnets 16, 26, 52, 68, 70, 78, 126.

CXXVI.

O thou, my lovely boy, who in thy power
Dost hold Time's fickle glass, his sickle, hour;
Who hast by waning grown, and therein show'st
Thy lovers withering, as thy sweet self grow'st;
If Nature, sovereign mistress over wrack,
As thou goest onwards, still will pluck thee back,
She keeps thee to this purpose, that her skill
May time disgrace, and wretched minutes kill.
Yet fear her, O thou minion of her pleasure!
She may detain, but not still keep, her treasure:
Her audit, though delay'd, answer'd must be,
And her quietus is to render thee.

Vide Sonnets 11, 125.

CXXVII.

In the old age black was not counted fair,
Or if it were, it bore not beauty's name;
But now is black beauty's successive heir,
And beauty slander'd with a bastard shame:
For since each hand hath put on nature's power,
Fairing the foul with art's false borrow'd face,
Sweet beauty hath no name, no holy bower,
But is profan'd, if not lives in disgrace.
Therefore' my mistress' eyes are raven black,
Her eyes so suited; and they mourners seem
At such, who, not born fair, no beauty lack,
Slandering creation with a false esteem:
    Yet so they mourn, becoming of their woe,
    That every tongue says, beauty should look·so.

Vide REMARKS, p. 57   also Sonnets 67, 78, 104, 132.

CXXVIII.

How oft, when thou, my music, music play'st,
Upon that blessed wood whose motion sounds
With thy sweet fingers, when thou gently sway'st
The wiry concord that mine ear confounds,
Do I envy those jacks that nimble leap
To kiss the tender inward of thy hand,
Whilst my poor lips, which should that harvest reap,
At the wood's boldness by thee blushing stand!
To be so tickled, they would change their state
And situation with those dancing chips,
O'er whom thy fingers walk with gentle gait,
Making dead wood more bless'd than living lips.
　　Since saucy jacks so happy are in this,
　　Give them thy fingers, me thy lips to kiss.

Vide REMARKS, p. 58.

CXXIX.

The expense of spirit in a waste of shame
Is lust in action; and till action, lust
Is perjur'd, murderous, bloody, full of blame,
Savage, extreme, rude, cruel, not to trust;
Enjoy'd no sooner, but despised straight;
Past reason hunted; and no sooner had,
Past reason hated, as a swallow'd bait,
On purpose laid to make the taker mad:
Mad in pursuit, and in possession so;
Had, having, and in quest to have, extreme;
A bliss in proof,—and prov'd, a very woe;
Before, a joy propos'd; behind, a dream.

    All this the world well knows; yet none knows well
    To shun the heaven that leads men to this hell.

Vide REMARKS, p. 59.

CXXX.

My mistress' eyes are nothing like the sun;
Coral is far more red than her lips' red:
If snow be white, why then her breasts are dun;
If hairs be wires, black wires grow on her head.
I have seen roses damask'd, red and white,
But no such roses see I in her cheeks;
And in some perfumes is there more delight
Than in the breath that from my mistress reeks,
I love to hear her speak,—yet well I know
That music hath a far more pleasing sound:
I grant I never saw a goddess go,—
My mistress, when she walks, treads on the ground.
    And yet, by heaven, I think my love as rare
    As any she belied with false compare.

CXXXI.

Thou art as tyrannous, so as thou art,
As those whose beauties proudly make them cruel;
For well thou know'st to my dear doting heart
Thou art the fairest and most precious jewel.
Yet, in good faith, some say that thee behold,
Thy face hath not the power to make love groan:
·To say they err, I dare not be so bold,
Although I swear it to myself alone.
And, to be sure that is not false I swear,
A thousand groans, but thinking on thy face,
One on another's neck, do witness bear
Thy black is fairest in my judgment's place.

  In nothing art thou black, save in thy deeds,
  And thence this slander, as I think, proceeds.

Vide Sonnet 27.

CXXXII.

Thine eyes I love, and they, as pitying me,
Knowing thy heart torments me with disdain,
Have put on black, and loving mourners be,
Looking with pretty ruth upon my pain.
And truly not the morning sun of heaven
Better becomes the grey cheeks of the east,
Nor that full star that ushers in the even
Doth half that glory to the sober west,
As those two mourning eyes become thy face:
O, let it, then, as well beseem thy heart
To mourn for me, since mourning doth thee grace,
And suit thy pity like in every part.

    Then will I swear beauty herself is black,
    And all they foul that thy complexion lack.

Vide Sonnet 127.

CXXXIII.

Beshrew that heart that makes my heart to groan
For that deep wound it gives my friend and me!
Is 't not enough to torture me alone,
But slave to slavery my sweet'st friend must be?
Me from myself thy cruel eye hath taken,
And my next self thou harder hast engross'd:
Of him, myself, and thee, I am forsaken;
A torment thrice three-fold thus to be cross'd.
Prison my heart in thy steel bosom's ward,
But then my friend's heart let my poor heart bail;
Who e'er keeps me, let my heart be his guard;
Thou canst not then use rigour in my gaol:
 And yet thou wilt; for I, being pent in thee,
 Perforce am thine, and all that is in me.

Vide REMARKS, pp. 41, 42: also Sonnet 147.

CXXXIV.

So, now I have confess'd that he is thine
And I myself am mortgag'd to thy will,
Myself I 'll forfeit, so that other mine
Thou wilt restore, to be my comfort still
But thou wilt not, nor he will not be free,
For thou art covetous, and he is kind;
He learn'd but, surety-like, to write for me,
Under that bond that him as fast doth bind.
The statute of thy beauty thou wilt take,
Thou usurer, that putt'st forth all to use,
And sue a friend, came debtor for my sake;
So him I lose through my unkind abuse.

    Him have I lost; thou hast both him and me:
    He pays the whole, and yet am I not free.

Vide REMARKS, p. 41 : also Sonnets 39, 42, 56, 142.

CXXXV.

Whoever hath her wish, thou hast thy *Will*,
And *Will* to boot, and *Will* in over-plus;
More than enough am I that vex thee still,
To thy sweet will making addition thus.
Wilt thou, whose will is large and spacious,
Not once vouchsafe to hide my will in thine?
Shall will in others seem right gracious,
And in my will no fair acceptance shine?
The sea, all water, yet receives rain still,
And in abundance addeth to his store;
So thou, being rich in *Will*, add to thy *Will*
One will of mine, to make thy large *Will* more.
    Let no unkind, no fair beseechers kill;
    Think all but one, and me in that one *Will.*

Vide REMARKS, pp. 43, 50, 51 · also Sonnets 40, 42.

CXXXVI.

If thy soul check thee that I come so near,
Swear to thy blind soul that I was thy *Will*,
And will, thy soul knows, is admitted there;
Thus far for love, my love-suit, sweet, fulfil.
Will will fulfil the treasure of thy love,
Ay, fill it full with wills, and my will one.
In things of great receipt with ease we prove,
Among a number one is reckon'd none:
Then in the number let me pass untold,
Though in thy stores' account I one must be;
For nothing hold me, so it please thee hold
That nothing me, a something sweet to thee:
    Make but my name thy love, and love that still,
    And then thou lov'st me,—for my name is *Will.*

Vide REMARKS, pp. 50, 51   also Sonnets 40, 143.

CXXXVII.

Thou blind fool, Love, what dost thou to mine eyes,
That they behold, and see not what they see?
They know what beauty is, see where it lies,
Yet what the best is, take the worst to be.
If eyes, corrupt by over-partial looks,
Be anchor'd in the bay where all men ride,
Why of eyes' falsehood hast thou forged hooks,
Whereto the judgment of my heart is tied?
Why should my heart think that a several plot,
Which my heart knows the wide world's common place?
Or mine eyes, seeing this, say this is not,
To put fair truth upon so foul a face?

 In things right true my heart and eyes have err'd,
 And to this false plague are they now transferr'd.

Vide Sonnets 113, 144, 147, 148, 150, 152.

11

CXXXVIII.

When my love swears that she is made of truth,
I do believe her, though I know she lies,
That she might think me some untutor'd youth,
Unlearned in the world's false subtleties.
Thus vainly thinking that she thinks me young,
Although she knows my days are past the best,
Simply I credit her false-speaking tongue:
On both sides thus is simple truth supprest.
But wherefore says she not she is unjust?
And wherefore say not I that I am old?
O, love's best habit is in seeming trust,
And age in love loves not to have years told:
 Therefore I lie with her, and she with me,
 And in our faults by lies we flatter'd be.

Vide REMARKS, p. 59 : also Sonnet 93.

CXXXIX.

O, call not me to justify the wrong
That thy unkindness lays upon my heart;
Wound me not with thine eye, but with thy tongue;
Use power with power, and slay me not by art.
Tell me thou lov'st elsewhere; but in my sight,
Dear heart, forbear to glance thine eye aside:
What need'st thou wound with cunning, when thy might
Is more than my o'erpress'd defence can 'bide?
Let me excuse thee: ah, my love well knows
Her pretty looks have been mine enemies;
And therefore from my face she turns my foes,
That they elsewhere might dart their injuries:

    Yet do not so; but since I am near slain,
    Kill me outright with looks, and rid my pain.

Vide Sonnet 41.

CXL.

Be wise as thou art cruel; do not press
My tongue-tied patience with too much disdain;
Lest sorrow lend me words, and words express
The manner of my pity-wanting pain.
If I might teach thee wit, better it were,
Though not to love, yet, love, to tell me so;—
As testy sick men, when their deaths be near,
No news but health from their physicians know;—
For, if I should despair, I should grow mad,
And in my madness might speak ill of thee:
Now this ill-wresting world is grown so bad,
Mad slanderers by mad ears believed be.

    That I may not be so, nor thou belied,
     Bear thine eyes straight, though thy proud heart go wide

Vide Sonnet 142.

CXLI.

In faith, I do not love thee with mine eyes,
For they in thee a thousand errors note;
But 't is my heart that loves what they despise,
Who, in despite of view, is pleas'd to dote;
Nor are mine ears with thy tongue's tune delighted·
Nor tender feeling, to base touches prone,
Nor taste, nor smell, desire to be invited
To any sensual feast with thee alone:
But my five wits, nor my five senses can
Dissuade one foolish heart from serving thee,
Who leaves unsway'd the likeness of a man,
Thy proud heart's slave and vassal wretch to be:
    Only my plague thus far I count my gain,
      That she that makes me sin, awards me pain.

Vide Sonnets 80, 150.

CXLII.

Love is my sin, and thy dear virtue hate,
Hate of my sin, grounded on sinful loving:
O, but with mine compare thou thine own state,
And thou shalt find it merits not reproving;
Or, if it do, not from those lips of thine,
That have profan'd their scarlet ornaments,
And seal'd false bonds of love as oft as mine,
Robb'd others' beds' revenues of their rents.
Be it lawful I love thee, as thou lov'st those
Whom thine eyes woo as mine importune thee:
Root pity in thy heart, that, when it grows,
Thy pity may deserve to pitied be.

    If thou dost seek to have what thou dost hide,
    By self-example may'st thou be denied!

Vide Sonnets 40, 140, 150.

CXLIII.

Lo, as a careful housewife runs to catch
One of her feather'd creatures broke away,
Sets down her babe, and makes all swift despatch
In pursuit of the thing she would have stay;
Whilst her neglected child holds her in chase,
Cries to catch her whose busy care is bent
To follow that which flies before her face,
Not prizing her poor infant's discontent:
So runn'st thou after that which flies from thee,
Whilst I thy babe chase thee afar behind;
But if thou catch thy hope, turn back to me,
And play the mother's part, kiss me, be kind:

    So will I pray that thou mayst have thy *Will*,
    If thou turn back, and my loud crying still.

Vide Sonnet 136.

CXLIV.

Two loves I have of comfort and despair,
Which like two spirits do suggest me still:
The better angel is a man right fair,
The worser spirit a woman colour'd ill.
To win me soon to hell, my female evil
Tempteth my better angel from my side,
And would corrupt my saint to be a devil,
Wooing his purity with her foul pride.
And whether that my angel be turn'd fiend,
Suspect I may, yet not directly tell;
But being both from me, both to each friend,
I guess one angel in another's hell:

> Yet this shall I ne'er know, but live in doubt,
> Till my bad angel fire my good one out.

Vide REMARKS, p. 36: also Sonnets 42, 137, 147.

CXLV.

Those lips that Love's own hand did make,
Breath'd forth the sound that said, "I hate,"
To me that languish'd for her sake:
But when she saw my woful state,
Straight in her heart did mercy come,
Chiding that tongue, that ever sweet
Was used in giving gentle doom;
And taught it thus anew to greet;
"I hate," she alter'd with an end,
That follow'd it as gentle day
Doth follow night, who, like a fiend,
From heaven to hell is flown away;
 "I hate" from hate away she threw,
 And sav'd my life, saying—"not you."

CXLVI.

Poor soul, the centre of my sinful earth,
Fool'd by these rebel powers that thee array,
Why dost thou pine within, and suffer dearth,
Painting thy outward walls so costly gay?
Why so large cost, having so short a lease,
Dost thou upon thy fading mansion spend?
Shall worms, inheritors of this excess,
Eat up thy charge? Is this thy body's end?
Then, soul, live thou upon thy servant's loss,
And let that pine to aggravate thy store;
Buy terms divine in selling hours of dross;
Within be fed, without be rich no more:
    So shalt thou feed on Death, that feeds on men,
    And, Death once dead, there 's no more dying then.

Vide REMARKS, pp. 60, 80 : also Sonnet 107.

CXLVII.

My love is as a fever, longing still
For that which longer nurseth the disease;
Feeding on that which doth preserve the ill,
The uncertain sickly appetite to please.
My reason, the physician to my love,
Angry that his prescriptions are not kept,
Hath left me, and I desperate now approve
Desire is death, which physic did except.
Past cure I am, now reason is past care,
And frantic mad with evermore unrest;
My thoughts and my discourse as mad men's are,
At random from the truth vainly express'd;

    For I have sworn thee fair, and thought thee bright,
    Who art as black as hell, as dark as night.

Vide REMARKS, pp. 37, 39, 60: also Sonnets 42, 119, 133, 137, 144.

CXLVIII.

O me, what eyes hath Love put in my head,
Which have no correspondence with true sight!
Or, if they have, where is my judgment fled,
That censures falsely what they see aright?
If that be fair whereon my false eyes dote,
What means the world to say it is not so?
If it be not, then love doth well denote
Love's eye is not so true as all men's: no,
How can it? O, how can Love's eye be true,
That is so vex'd with watching and with tears?
No marvel, then, though I mistake my view;
The sun itself sees not, till heaven clears.

　　O cunning Love! with tears thou keep'st me blind,
　　Lest eyes well-seeing thy foul faults should find.

Vide Sonnets 113, 137.

CXLIX.

Canst thou, O cruel! say I love thee not,
When I, against myself, with thee partake?
Do I not think on thee, when I forgot
Am of myself, all tyrant, for thy sake?
Who hateth thee that I do call my friend?
On whom frown'st thou that I do fawn upon?
Nay, if thou low'rst on me, do I not spend
Revenge upon myself with present moan?
What merit do I in myself respect,
That is so proud thy service to despise,
When all my best doth worship thy defect,
Commanded by the motion of thine eyes?
    But, love, hate on, for now I know thy mind;
    Those that can see thou lov'st, and I am blind.

Vide REMARKS, p. 62 : also Sonnets 88, 89.

CL.

O, from what power hast thou this powerful might,
With insufficiency my heart to sway?
To make me give the lie to my true sight,
And swear that brightness doth not grace the day?
Whence hast thou this becoming of things ill,
That in the very refuse of thy deeds
There is such strength and warrantise of skill,
That, in my mind, thy worst all best exceeds?
Who taught thee how to make me love thee more,
The more I hear 'and see just cause of hate?
O, though I love what others do abhor,
With others thou shouldst not abhor my state:

    If thy unworthiness rais'd love in me,
    More worthy I to be belov'd of thee.

Vide REMARKS, pp. 62, 64 : also Sonnets 15, 16, 27, 57, 58, 89, 95, 96, 113, 120, 137, 142, 148.

CLI.

Love is too young to know what conscience is;
Yet who knows not, conscience is born of love?
Then, gentle cheater, urge not my amiss,
Lest guilty of my faults thy sweet self prove.
For, thou betraying me, I do betray
My nobler part to my gross body's treason;
My soul doth tell my body that he may
Triumph in love; flesh stays no farther reason;
But, rising at thy name, doth point out thee
As his triumphant prize. Proud of 'this pride,
He is contented thy poor drudge to be,
To stand in thy affairs, fall by thy side.

No want of conscience hold it that I call
Her "love," for whose dear love I rise and fall.

Vide Sonnet 150.

CLII.

In loving thee thou know'st I am forsworn,
But thou art twice forsworn, to me love swearing;
In act thy bed-vow broke, and new faith torn,
In vowing new hate after new love bearing.
But why of two oaths' breach do I accuse thee,
When I break twenty?   I am perjur'd most;
For all my vows are oaths but to misuse thee,
And all my honest faith in thee is lost:
For I have sworn deep oaths of thy deep kindness,
Oaths of thy love, thy truth, thy constancy;
And, to enlighten thee, gave eyes to blindness,
Or made them swear against the thing they see;

    For I have sworn thee fair,—more perjur'd I,
    To swear, against the truth, so foul a lie!

Vide Sonnets 41, 69, 87, 88, 137.

CLIII.

Cupid laid by his brand, and fell asleep:
A maid of Dian's this advantage found,
And his love-kindling fire did quickly steep
In a cold valley-fountain of that ground;
Which borrow'd from this holy fire of Love
A dateless lively heat, still to endure,
And grew a seething bath, which yet men prove
Against strange maladies a sovereign cure.
But at my mistress' eye Love's brand new-fir'd,
The boy for trial needs would touch my breast;
I, sick withal, the help of bath desir'd,
And thither hied, a sad distemper'd guest,
    But found no cure: the bath for my help lies
    Where Cupid got new fire,—my mistress' eyes.

Vide REMARKS, pp. 47, 66, 89 : also Sonnets 24, 122.

CLIV.

The little Love-god, lying once asleep,
Laid by his side his heart-inflaming brand,
Whilst many nymphs that vow'd chaste life to keep
Came tripping by; but in her maiden hand
The fairest votary took up that fire
Which many legions of true hearts had warm'd;
And so the general of hot desire
Was, sleeping, by a virgin hand disarm'd.
This brand she quenched in a cool well by,
Which from Love's fire took heat perpetual,
Growing a bath and healthful remedy
For men diseas'd; but I, my mistress' thrall,
    Came there for cure, and this by that I prove,
    Love's fire heats water, water cools not love.

Vide REMARKS, p. 66 : also Sonnets 24, 122.

CHAPTER VIII.

THE author of the Remarks on the Sonnets of
Shakespeare thinks the question discussed in those
remarks of sufficient importance to justify some further attempt to confirm the view therein presented,
his attention having been called to a few of the sonnets supposed to present special difficulties not fully
explained.   He, therefore, makes the following addi-
tional remarks and explanations; and, first, in reference to the 67th and 68th Sonnets, which read:

> 67. Ah, wherefore, &c.
> 68. Thus is his cheek, &c.

The poet of the Sonnets, after stating a mere possibility in the 104th Sonnet, concludes with the two
following lines:

> 104. For fear of which, hear this, thou age unbred,—
> Ere you were born was beauty's summer dead.

These lines were addressed to the " age " in which the poet lived, and that age he calls "unbred," evidently meaning uncultivated, in comparison with some preceding age, which he as evidently refers to in the last line of the sonnet as " Beauty's Summer."

That the reference is to some former age, by the designation of it as Beauty's Summer, may be seen by the closing lines of the 67th Sonnet, without pointing out other evidences, thus:

> 67. O, *him* she stores, to show what wealth she had
>   In days long since, before these last so bad.

The reference here (to "him ") is to the object addressed by the poet of the sonnets, under a figure, in the 1st Sonnet, as " Beauty's Rose "; but which in the 20th Sonnet is called the " Master-Mistress of the poet's passion (or love); and this, we say, is not a person, but a mystical expression for an object conceived as double, masculine and feminine in one, which object, being thus conceived, the poet sometimes addresses in the masculine and sometimes in the feminine gender. He sometimes speaks as if to the object, and at times to each part separately, and sometimes he makes one part, as it were, address another, as in Sonnets 151, 136, 42, 146, 144, 46, 47,

&c., &c., telling us in Sonnet 105 what "wondrous scope" he finds in those "three themes in one" (only varying the "words")—the poet himself making one of the three,—in which, as he says, his "invention is spent."

In this 67th Sonnet the language, "him she stores," is to be understood by considering the spirit as the masculine side of nature, the latter being the feminine side, the one being stable, the other changeable (though changing according to the law of the fixed), while each, nevertheless, derives a certain *relative* character from the other, which enables the poet to refer to the masculine as having been "stored" with qualities by the feminine, or nature side of life; and hence he says here that *she*, or nature, has stored *him*, the conceived "lovely boy" (Sonnet 126), "to show what wealth she had in days long since, before these last so bad,"—and the "him" here is no other than what we may call the genius or inspiration, or the Muse of the poet, of whose possession and power he was conscious. The poet, in other words, felt that he had been endowed with the so-called "gift" of poetic genius, which, while he considered it the "better part" of himself (Sonnet 39), was, nevertheless, acknowledged as a pure grace, as shown in Sonnet

87. This is what the poet considered had been stored" with nature's power, as if to show to the poet himself what wealth she formerly had, that is, in some "age" preceding that in which the poet lived and characterizes as "unbred."

In the 83d Sonnet the poet refers to the *object* addressed as being *extant*, as if for the same purpose, that of enabling him to judge (line 7, Sonnet 83) "how far a modern quill" fell short of the beauty which, he saw, had been the inspiration of some preceding age. In the 84th Sonnet the same object is called an *example*, in the sense of an exemplar or pattern, by which to make the same judgment, upon a comparison of the poet's age with some preceding age, in which beauty is said to have had its summer.

A similar idea may be seen in the 127th Sonnet, the first line of which reads :

127. In the old age *black* was not counted *fair* :

meaning that, in some preceding age, doubtless referring to that which, in the 104th Sonnet, is called "beauty's summer," *evil* was not counted *good;* and, as a consequence, the poet saw that, in the old age (the golden age), "Beauty lived and died," as he says

in the second line of the 68th Sonnet, as naturally as
"flowers" in his own "age unbred."

To show, now, what "age" is referred to, when
beauty lived and died as naturally as "flowers," we
refer to the 108th Sonnet, where we see that love—
and love, in the sonnets, is synonymous with beauty
—is called "eternal love;" and we are told that eternal love does not *weigh* (that is, it does not consider
or is not *impeded* by) the "dust and injury of age,"
and gives "no place to necessary wrinkles" (having,
itself, what is called in Sonnet 18 an eternal summer,
meaning an eternal youth); but, says the poet,
"makes antiquity for aye his page;" or, in other
words, the spirit of love (or beauty) makes the classics
of *antiquity* a study, because, says the poet, it finds
there the "first conceit of love" (or beauty), "where
time and outward form would show it dead."

That is, the poet, in his "true love" (line 9, Sonnet 21), looked backward in time beyond his own
"unbred" age into the classics of antiquity, where
he saw the first conceit of love, or of that beauty
which was the object of his own "passion;"—not a
person in any proper sense, though manifested in
persons, but the beautiful in the Platonic sense, or in
that of the Canticles; for, let the reader think what

he may, a divine spirit of beauty is surely the inspiration of the Song of Songs, where a curious eye may detect the Master-Mistress of our poet.

We say that love and beauty are synonymous expressions in the Sonnets (though somewhat as truth and goodness are one), because love and its object are, in a certain sense, one; and they are perpetually conceived as one when both, the love and the beauty, are conceived as eternal; and here we have two elements, so to say, of the eternal trinity, the third being the love of the poet himself when directed to the Master-Mistress, or love and beauty; where we must see also the "fair, kind, and true" of the 105th Sonnet; which are only "other words" for the beautiful, the good, and the true—three themes in one, says our poet, which wondrous scope affords, and in which his invention was exhausted, as he tells us himself.

Again: the poet, we say, makes an evident comparison between the age which, in the 104th Sonnet, he calls the "summer of beauty," and his own unbred age, very greatly to the disadvantage of the age in which he lived, in which, as he tells us in the 68th Sonnet, he saw only what he calls "bastard signs of fair," that is, of beauty; and the poet, in this 68th Sonnet, accuses his own age of seeking to ornament itself by appropriating what he calls the "golden tresses of the dead," plainly meaning that, in his time, it was customary for poets to appropriate the beauties of the classics, to embellish with them their own "living brows," calling those plagiarized beauties the "dead fleece" of beauty, &c., and beauty, thus used, is described, in line 10, Sonnet 67, as "blushing" through the lively (or living) veins of the poets of his own day—an idea which may be observed in several of the Sonnets of our poet.

The reader may readily find some confirmation of this view by looking at the Elizabethan literature just prior to the appearance of our poet upon the stage of life; for it was the culminating period of the revival of literature, when the ancient classics were everywhere studied and translated into modern languages. The literary practices of that period furnished the materials for Dean Swift's humorous Essay to prove that the ancients stole all their thoughts from the moderns.

The poet assigns as a reason for the low state of literature prior, as we must say, to his own time, this "bastard" use of what he calls beauty's "dead fleece" —explaining that this was owing to the fact that "each hand" (line 5, Sonnet 127), meaning that every

23

writer had "put on," or attempted to use, what he
calls "nature's power,"—the same explanation for the
same fact being referred to in the last line of the 69th
Sonnet, where he says that "him," meaning the
spirit, or spirit side of nature, or nature's power, had
grown "common;" or, in other words again, that
every common writer, in his time, was attempting to
use nature's power; which was, in fact, no other than
the object of his own passion—the Master-Mistress of
the 20th Sonnet being an expression for nature, seen
in her beauty and power, under the figurative expression of Beauty's Rose: for it is designated by
many *words*, as we read in Sonnet 105.

We lose the characteristics of the universal when
we put limitations upon it and define it as having
this or that significance exclusively, expressed by the
sense of any one word.   The Rose is true, or truth;
it is also the beautiful and the good; and it is power
no less: it was to the poet all in all, as we read in
the 109th Sonnet:

> 109. Never believe, though in my nature reigned
>   All frailties that besiege all kinds of blood,
>   That I could so preposterously be stained,
>   To leave for nothing all thy sum of good;
>   For nothing this wide universe I call,   •
>   Save thou, my Rose; in it thou art my all.

We return now to the 67th Sonnet, and observe that the language, "O, him she stores," &c., refers to the spirit of Beauty, as being "stored" by nature in its own unparticipated simplicity, which evinced to the poet, who saw it in that simplicity, the *wealth* she had long before his own age, the poet looking at the past through a historic vision; and then follows Sonnet 68 (the explanation of which is the immediate object of this chapter):

> 67. Thus is his *cheek* the map of days outworn, &c.

which signifies that the poet saw, in the history of the past, what he calls the "cheek" or outside of that beauty which was the object of his own passion; and that beauty he saw in nature, not as she is visible which is but the cheek of nature, but as she is conceived in her spirit; and that spirit the poet calls, in line 9, Sonnet 69, the Beauty of Mind.

In the 69th Sonnet, however, the poet acknowledges or affirms the beauty and perfection of nature, both as visible and invisible, when seen in and for itself simply, his complaint being that it was looked at in what he calls "guess;" whereas, as he tells us in Sonnet 84, it is only necessary to be simply true; urging that nature should be shown to be just what she is, without "bastard" attempts at embellishment by robbing "golden fleeces" from a dead antiquity, which he calls, in Sonnet 127, "fairing the foul with art's false borrowed face."

"He that writes of you," says our poet, addressing the spirit of beauty, or the spirit of nature, "let him but copy what in you is writ, not making worse what nature made so clear, and such a counterpart shall fame his wit," &c., and this, in our poet's view, was what he calls, in Hamlet, "holding the mirror up to nature."

This is also the theme of the 83d Sonnet:

83. I never saw that you did painting need, &c.

which the poet might have had in mind when he exclaimed, "Who can paint the lily, or throw a perfume on the violet," &c.

In short, the poet himself was his "mother's glass" (Sonnet 3), and she in him "called back the lovely

April of her prime," where she saw, or enables us to see, "beauty's summer," as revived in our poet.

The poet of the Sonnets, we repeat, did not address a person in those wonderful productions, but gave expression, in a series of monologues, to his own contemplations upon nature, as seen in the spirit of "beauty, truth, and rarity."

CHAPTER IX.

THE 142d Sonnet has been pointed out as especially difficult of interpretation; but it falls very decidedly within the scope of the author's theory.

142. Love is my sin, &c.

In order to explain the meaning of this Sonnet, we again refer to the 87th Sonnet, beginning:

87. Farewell! thou art too dear for my possessing, &c.

which closes with the lines:

Thus have I had thee, as a dream doth flatter
In sleep a king, but, waking, no such matter.

If the reader will but look into the poets, he will find, with nearly all of them, certainly the best of them, abundant reason to understand that the divine afflatus, or poetic gift, however " constant " in itself,

is not only a gift, in its origin, in each poet, but its
stay with the poet is not subject to the control of the
poet himself.   Of this may be said what is said of the
spirit of religion : " The wind bloweth as it listeth,
and thou hearest the sound thereof, but canst not tell
whence it cometh or whither it goeth."

If we apply this to the poetic gift or genius, it is
exactly true, and hence comes the saying, that a poet
is not made, but born.

We would ask the reader to consider this point
closely, and then observe the language of the 87th
Sonnet, where we think he must see that the poet, in
that sonnet, is addressing what we may call the poetic
gift, which the poet acknowledges he held only by·
its own "granting;" not finding in himself the *desert*
which could be considered as giving him a claim to
it.   "The cause," says he, "of this *fair gift* in me is
wanting;" and he concludes by expressing the sad
conviction that, in its possession, he had been blessed
but as in a dream, discovering the illusion upon being
awakened, as it were, from a dream.

Unless the reader accepts this view he will not be
likely to follow the inferences to be made from it.
Our poet understood the poet's elevation perfectly
when he tells us of the poet's eye as " in a fine frenzy

rolling," etc.; and Shelley's Ode to Intellectual Beauty will show the depths of the darkness into which the poet falls when deserted by the inspiration.

Now, it is important to bear in mind that the poetic gift abandons those who in any manner abuse it, or employ it upon unsuitable or unworthy subjects. It is in its own nature purity itself, and allows no unclean thing to come near or contaminate it. This is the next point to be accepted as indisputable, and the reader will then be prepared to understand the 100th Sonnet, which begins:

> 100. Where art thou, Muse, that thou forgett'st so long
>   To speak of *that* which gives thee all thy might ?

This is a rebuke of the poet himself (by himself) for not holding fast the spirit of beauty which had been the fountain of his inspiration; and then, as if he understood something of the reason for its absence, he asks:

> Spend'st thou thy fury on some worthless song,
>   Dark'ning thy power, to lend base subjects light ?

—the remainder of the sonnet being a further commentary upon the purity and perpetuity of the spirit of beauty, as it is in itself; upon which Time, as the poet says or implies, can write no "wrinkle," while yet the poet, as we see, felt or knew that he could "darken" its power by employing it unworthily.

In the New Melusina of Meister's Travels there is a perfect illustration of this point, where the hero of the story represents himself as seeking "companions at tables d'hote, in coffee-houses, and public places" —in forgetfulness of his Beauty, precisely the Beauty seen by the poet of the Sonnets; and then he says: "In such a mode of living my *money* [by which he figures the poetic gift] began to melt away; and one night it vanished entirely from my purse in a fit of passionate gaming, which I had not had the prudence to abandon."

The curious reader may find many parallels in the story of the New Melusina illustrative of the Sonnets, for that story is a symbolic history of genius. The several *quarrels* exhibited in the story were intended to illustrate the experiences of a poet, or of any artist indeed—his hopes and fears, his raptures, despondency, doubts, alarms, &c. The scene in which Meister is shown as having been captivated by a "couple of ladies," at the close of which his personified genius bids "farewell to Moroseness and Caprice," is beautifully symbolical ; the *two* ladies representing the ever-recurring *two* in hermetic writings—any two illusory attractions.

We must now consider that our poet has been in the conscious possession of the poetic gift, but has found its possession disturbed by his own sense of having neglected his Muse—he had *forgotten* to speak of or to honor the gift—and his peace was disturbed also by the sense of having employed his inspiration in "lending base subjects light ;" and this is what he calls in the 142d Sonnet "sin" or "sinful loving."

To take the poet's meaning in the use of these expressions, we must observe that his *ideal* stands before his mind as the perfect, or, rather, as perfection itself; and this he regards as the principle of his life, to which he owes the most absolute fidelity. This is the principle which absorbs all his love (Sonnet 40), before which, as we see in many Sonnets, he bows in the most extreme humility, while he exults in its *light* and predicts the immortality of the verses inspired by it, and which he dedicates to it. This must explain the meaning of the first lines of the 26th Sonnet :

26. Lord of my love, to whom in vassalage
   Thy *merit* has my duty strongly knit,
   To thee I send this written embassage,
   To witness duty, not to show my wit; &c.

The *merit* contemplated by the poet is without
limit; and so, therefore, is his sense of "duty;" hence
his verses of praise were only regarded as attempts
to "witness duty," but on no account to show his
wit.

This being the poet's conception of the object addressed and of his duty to it, we may readily see that
sin or sinful loving, in the poet's use of these words,
cannot be regarded as any specific form of sin under
the current definitions of the world, but applies to
any and every, even the slightest, departure from the
highest conceivable sense of duty to the absolutely
perfect.

Among the duties of the poet under the conception we indicate, must be included the sense of
obligation he felt of *praise*, the language of the 39th
Sonnet; and this will show us the meaning of the
23d Sonnet, where the poet represents himself as
"forgetting to say the perfect ceremony of love's
rite;" which signifies that he cannot adequately

praise what he conceives to be above all praise; and this, as he elsewhere says, is what makes his verse as but a " tomb " (Sonnets 17, 83) of the perfect beauty he contemplated; and he asks, or we may say he prays, that the object addressed might read (or accept) what his " silent love " hath writ, using the figure that it belongs to love's fine wit to *hear* (that is, to understand), by what the eye sees of his verses, while these do but *entomb* the beauty they celebrate; except, as we may say, to those who the poet himself says have " lover's eyes " (Sonnet 55); for whose eyes, as the poet considered, the Beauty was but " ensconced " (Sonnet 49) in the Sonnets, or put under a slight hermetic veil, to be removed by those to whom the poet himself supposed he had given eyes (Sonnet 152).

Sin, therefore, in the sense of the poet, includes even the neglect of that duty of *praise* which the poet felt called upon to offer—" duty so great, [says he,] which wit so poor as mine

> 26. May make seem bare, in wanting words to show it."

We do not hesitate to say that the Psalms of David will furnish many verses explanatory of the state of mind of our poet, only we must observe,

that the poet had, in his aspirations, a worldly taint
unknown to the Psalmist, in that it was distinctly
his ambition to " write," though he desired to write
" truly " (Sonnet 21) ; for which purpose he sought
the direct inspiration of " truth in beauty dy'd."
(Sonnet 101).   Our poet was sensible of this ambi-
tious element in himself, and condemns it in the
147th Sonnet :

> 147. My love, [says he,] is as a fever, longing still
>   For that which longer nurseth the disease ;
>   Feeding on that which doth preserve the ill,
>   *The uncertain sickly appetite to please.*

It was the presence of these, as we may call them,
human tendencies, that disturbed the poet, for they
are incompatible with the pure ideal, or the ideal of
perfect purity.   Hence the rebuke of the poet to
himself, in Sonnet 101 :

> 101. O truant Muse, what shall be thy amends
>   [or, what amends can you make]
>   For thy neglect of truth in beauty dy'd ?

or, as in the 100th Sonnet :

24

100.   Where art thou, Muse, that thou forgett'st so long
          To speak of *that* which gives thee all thy might?
      Spend'st thou thy fury on some worthless song,
          Dark'ning thy power to lend base subjects light?

for truth in beauty dy'd is precisely that which gave
our poet all his power.

A right conception of the object addressed by
the poet, under the figure of Beauty's Rose, and a
proper understanding of these lines, will afford, with
the preceding explanations, the key to Sonnet 142,
in which the sin or sinful loving referred to is
not, as we have already said, any specific form of
worldly sin, but the reference is to the self-accusa-
tion of the poet for having neglected to offer the due
meed of *praise*, and for having profaned his gift by
employing it upon inferior or unworthy subjects.
Here we must see the kind of sinning referred to in
the Sonnet, as the structure of the Sonnet will
show.

The poet says, as if in defence of himself,

142.   O, but with mine compare thou thine own state,
      And thou shalt find it merits not reproving.

In these lines the poet points at the immeasura-
ble distance between himself as a mere man, a *worm*

of the dust, and the absolute perfection of the object addressed, which is conceived as perfection itself—so perfect, as the poet would infer, that it should make no account of his imperfections, somewhat in the style of the argument of the 136th Sonnet:

> 136. In things of great receipt with ease we prove,
>   Among a number one is reckon'd none.

And then he proceeds (Sonnet 142):

Or, if it do—that is, if the poet merits reproof, he argues that such reproof should not come (using figurative language):

> 142. * * —from those lips of thine,
>   That have profaned their scarlet ornaments,
>   And seal'd false bonds of love as oft as mine.

The argument of the poet is, we say, that if he merits reproof for having neglected the performance of the " perfect rite of love," or *praise,* the reproof should not come from the object addressed; because, first, of its own exceeding beauty, or perfection, which is so great as, by contrast or comparison, to make his own delinquencies, as it were, but as nothing; and then, secondly, because of its own illusory promises; which the poet means to say are

deceptive, inasmuch as they had raised in the poet
the most heavenly hopes, only to plunge him into
the deepest depths of darkness; its promises being
compared to " seal'd bonds of love."

The reader may here be referred to the last line
of the 22d Sonnet, in the writing of which the poet
must have thought he held his ideal secure against
all chances, as if under sacred promises, or *seal'd
bonds ;* while its absence, or its withdrawing itself,
(distinctly pointed at in the 87th Sonnet) is compared, in the 142d Sonnet, to robbing others' beds'
revenues of their rents ; which has no other meaning
than that poets (who are the *beds* wherein great
works of art are *conceived*) have been robbed or
cheated, as it were, out of their hopes of glory and
immortality, by the fact, that the "gift," upon
which their hopes had been founded, had been taken
away; the possibility of which is recognized also in
the 91st Sonnet, beginning,

91. Some glory in their birth, &c.,

in which the poet expresses his perfect joy in the
possession of the one "general best" (for there is
but one, and can be but one), only unhappy in that

the personified spirit of beauty might take all its gifts away, and thus make him "most wretched."

That this is the true interpretation is made still more plain by the two closing lines of the Sonnet, to wit:

142. If thou dost seek to *have* what thou dost *hide,* &c.

That is, if thou dost seek to have from the poet the praise which can only be the product of your own *light* in the soul, and yet dost "hide" that light, then, as the poet infers:

By self-example thou may'st be denied.

That is, plainly, the poet, as if in argument with the high ideal he addresses, and which he personifies for poetic purposes, contends that he may claim to be excused for having neglected the performance of the duty of *praise,* when the *light,* by which alone he can properly praise, is withheld; in which, as he urges, he but follows the self-example of his ideal Beauty, whose visitations he has now discovered to be transitory, illusive, or deceptive.

In all this, and in most of the Sonnets, the Spirit of Beauty is simply personified, and then the poet holds seeming intercourse and conferences with it.

24*

He glories in it; he praises it; he reasons with it; he deprecates its supposed anger; he complains of it, or of himself in relation to it; and yet he submits absolutely to it, as in the 89th and other Sonnets:

> 89. For thee, against myself, I'll vow debate,
>   For I must ne'er love him whom thou dost hate.

When the poet speaks of " sin," or of " sinning," therefore, we are not to infer a specific form of worldly sin. The Beauty the poet sees commands his love, and his entire love (see Sonnet 40); and it follows that to love any other object separated from *that*, in which he saw his " all " (Sonnet 109), is sin, precisely in accordance with the doctrine of the Scripture, where it is treated in the broadest language possible, as may be seen in the 16th chapter of Ezekiel, and in many other places, though it is commonly called going after false gods, where the language would as accurately express the truth, if it had been called going after false loves, all loves being false when pursued in oblivion of the one true love; which is no other than the love of God: and this, when truly conceived, is that love which St. John defines as God—the love and the object becoming one.

No ordinary metaphysics or dialectics can deal properly with this subject, not from any imperfection in reason itself, but from the absence in so many of us of the facts of the soul necessary to a complete view of the case, and hence it is that so many writers have, when treating of it, resorted to figurative and symbolical language—as in the Sonnets attributed to Shakespeare. It is doing but common justice to own that, in the composition of the Sonnets, the poet's imagination, or rather his whole soul, was so completely occupied with the pure ideal, that it never once occurred to him, that in his mode of treating it he was making himself obnoxious to accusations the most damaging to his reputation as a man; and it is high time that the reader of the Sonnets should be confronted with the maxim, *honi soit qui mal pense.*

Before closing this chapter the author of the Remarks observes, that the 152d Sonnet must have been written when the poet was under the most painful sense of his liability to lose the influence of the ideal, as we may see in the 87th Sonnet. Several of the Remarks in this and the preceding chapter will readily suggest explanations of this 152d Son-

net. The poet, in the opening lines of the Sonnet,
accuses his Muse of having been " twice forsworn."
This means that, after first raising high hopes in him,
as we may see in the 22d Sonnet, it had so far with-
drawn itself as to produce the distress indicated in
several of the Sonnets preceding the 119th, in which
he celebrates the renewal of his love.

> 119. O benefit of ill ! [says he,] now I find true
>   That better is by evil still made better ;
>   And ruin'd love, when it is built anew,
>   Grows fairer than at first, more strong, far greater.
>   So I return rebuked to my content,
>   And gain by ill thrice more than I have spent.

Another, a second departure of the ideal, after
this renewal of love, furnished the ground of the
second line of the 152d Sonnet :

> 152. Thou art twice forsworn, to me love swearing, &c.

The allusion to the " bed-vow " in the third line,
has the sense already given (in this chapter) to the
eighth line of the 142d Sonnet, the poet himself
being the *bed* in which the ideal, the Muse, had im-
pressed upon him the conviction of her truth and
power, and which he figuratively calls a vow—a

" bed-vow "—which, in his new distress, he says, has
been broken a second time: but then the poet accuses himself as the "most perjured," feeling that
all of his vows were but oaths to misuse the Rose,
or the perfect Beauty which he contemplated; which
can have no other meaning, than that all of his vows,
in reference to his Muse, contained in them some
attribute or element out of harmony with that singleness of devotion which, in principle, the pure ideal
demands. The unparticipated nature of the Rose is
such, that, in a strict sense, as it is above all praise,
so it rejects all service, having in view any other
object than itself; and especially does it reject a
service contaminated with an "uncertain sickly ap
petite to please" the world (Sonnet 147).

The poet deeply laments his self-love; for whï
his conception of the ideal required its destructioi
there was in him too much of the merely human, to
permit his perfect success, in his effort to come into
conformity with his theory. He says, in Sonnet 62,

> 62. Sin of self-love possesser all mine eye,
> And all my soul, and all my every part;
> And for this sin there is no remedy,
> It is so grounded inward in my heart.

Even when praising the *perfect*, he did so under

a sense of its being his own "better part" (Sonnet
39), and hence he says, Sonnet 62,

> 'Tis thee (myself) that for myself I praise,
> Painting my age with beauty of thy days.

We must see, in the 152d Sonnet, that the poet's
experience of the illusory promises of the ideal (due
to his own fault, however) had fully prepared him to
look to the Law for strength and support, as shown
in the two closing Sonnets of the series, which are
interpreted in pp. 45-49 of the Remarks, in connection with what is said of the 122d Sonnet.

On the whole, the reader of the Sonnets of
Shakespeare must, we think, make up his mind that
the object addressed was not a person, except where
the poet addresses himself; and the object was and
is invisible, except as to what every man may see for
himself now "extant" (Sonnet 83);—but it has its
residence in a secret "closet, never pierced with crys
tal eyes" (Sonnet 46).

Trieste

Trieste Publishing has a massive catalogue of classic book titles. Our aim is to provide readers with the highest quality reproductions of fiction and non-fiction literature that has stood the test of time. The many thousands of books in our collection have been sourced from libraries and private collections around the world.

The titles that Trieste Publishing has chosen to be part of the collection have been scanned to simulate the original. Our readers see the books the same way that their first readers did decades or a hundred or more years ago. Books from that period are often spoiled by imperfections that did not exist in the original. Imperfections could be in the form of blurred text, photographs, or missing pages. It is highly unlikely that this would occur with one of our books. Our extensive quality control ensures that the readers of Trieste Publishing's books will be delighted with their purchase. Our staff has thoroughly reviewed every page of all the books in the collection, repairing, or if necessary, rejecting titles that are not of the highest quality. This process ensures that the reader of one of Trieste Publishing's titles receives a volume that faithfully reproduces the original, and to the maximum degree possible, gives them the experience of owning the original work.

We pride ourselves on not only creating a pathway to an extensive reservoir of books of the finest quality, but also providing value to every one of our readers. Generally, Trieste books are purchased singly - on demand, however they may also be purchased in bulk. Readers interested in bulk purchases are invited to contact us directly to enquire about our tailored bulk rates. Email: customerservice@triestepublishing.com

You May Also Like

Results of Astronomical Observations Made at the Sydney Observatory, New South Wales, in the Years 1877 and 1878

H. C. Russell

ISBN: 9780649692613
Paperback: 120 pages
Dimensions: 6.14 x 0.25 x 9.21 inches
Language: eng

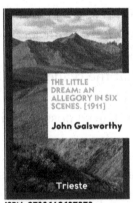

The Little Dream: An Allegory in Six Scenes. [1911]

John Galsworthy

ISBN: 9780649637270
Paperback: 50 pages
Dimensions: 6.14 x 0.10 x 9.21 inches
Language: eng

www.triestepublishing.com

You May Also Like

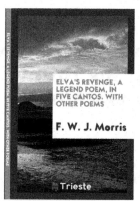

ELva's Revenge, a Legend Poem, in Five Cantos. With Other Poems

F. W. J. Morris

ISBN: 9780649573073
Paperback: 146 pages
Dimensions: 6.14 x 0.31 x 9.21 inches
Language: eng

Persecution and Tolerance: Being the Hulsean Lectures Preached Before the University of Cambridge in 1893-4

Mandell Creighton

ISBN: 9780649669356
Paperback: 164 pages
Dimensions: 6.14 x 0.35 x 9.21 inches
Language: eng

www.triestepublishing.com

You May Also Like

ISBN: 9780649420544
Paperback: 108 pages
Dimensions: 6.14 x 0.22 x 9.21 inches
Language: eng

1807-1907 The One Hundredth Anniversary of the incorporation of the Town of Arlington Massachusetts

Various

ISBN: 9780649194292
Paperback: 44 pages
Dimensions: 6.14 x 0.09 x 9.21 inches
Language: eng

Biennial report of the Board of Stat Harbor Commissioners, for the two fiscal years commencing July 1, 1890, and ending June 30, 1892

Various

www.triestepublishing.com

You May Also Like

ISBN: 9780649199693
Paperback: 48 pages
Dimensions: 6.14 x 0.10 x 9.21 inches
Language: eng

Biennial report of the Board of State Harbor Commissioners for the two fisca years. Commeneing July 1, 1884, and Ending June 30, 1886

Various

ISBN: 9780649196395
Paperback: 44 pages
Dimensions: 6.14 x 0.09 x 9.21 inches
Language: eng

Biennial report of the Board of state commissioners, for the two fiscal years, commencing July 1, 1890, and ending June 30, 1892

Various

Find more of our titles on our website. We have a selection of thousands of titles that will interest you. Please visit

www.triestepublishing.com

Lightning Source UK Ltd.
Milton Keynes UK
UKOW06f0942231017
311488UK00005B/896/P